...

THE DESIGN WAY

...

Intentional Change
in an
Unpredictable World

...

FOUNDATIONS AND FUNDAMENTALS OF DESIGN COMPETENCE

Harold G. Nelson
Erik Stolterman

Educational Technology Publications
Englewood Cliffs, New Jersey 07632

Cover design by Harold G. Nelson.

Library of Congress Cataloging-in-Publication Data

Nelson, Harold G.
 The design way : intentional change in an unpredictable world :
foundations and fundamentals of design competence / Harold G. Nelson,
Erik Stolterman.
  p. cm.
Includes bibliographical references and index.
 ISBN 0-87778-305-5
 1. Design–Philosophy. 2. System design. 3. Design–Study and
teaching. I. Stolterman, Erik. II. Title.
 NK1505.N43 2003
 745.4'01–dc21

                                                    2002192836

Printed in the United States of America.

Library of Congress Catalog Card Number:
2002192836.

International Standard Book Number:
0-87778-305-5.

First Printing: May, 2003.

This book is dedicated to:

Anne, Autumn, Erikka, Evelyn
Maria, Adam, Ludvig

Table of Contents

Table of Figures

ix

Acknowledgments

Many people have helped us in developing both the content of this book and its form. We owe them a great deal and would like to give them our thanks for their friendship, support and professionalism. We have had the chance to work with a number of colleagues in different design fields over the years. Their questions, thoughts and ideas have greatly helped us to formulate our own composition. But, since our work on the book has been going on for quite some time, we know that we cannot acknowledge all of you, who in one way or another contributed to this final version of the book. So, to all of you: Thanks!

We are deeply thankful to our students, both in the United States and in Sweden, who have helped us by reading earlier versions, asking questions, being honestly critical of ideas, but especially for encouraging us to go on with our work.

We want to thank the following individuals and organizations specifically. We would like to thank our colleague and friend Bob Sandusky, co-founder and officer in the Advanced Design Institute. We also want to send our thanks to Elizabeth Heffron for her invaluable insights, guidance and support in crafting the final text. We would also like to thank Torbjörn Nordström, Anna Croon Fors, Kristo Ivanov, Jonas Löwgren and Lawrence Lipsitz for their willingness to read, reflect and comment on earlier versions of this text. In addition, we would like to thank Anne Nelson for her assistance with the early drafts as well as with the final drafting of our manuscript. Her energy and support were the constants we came to depend on. Finally, we would like to thank those who read and commented on our final draft of the manuscript: Russell Ackoff, Tom Fisher, Russell Osguthorpe, Jim Platts and Gordon Rowland.

We also want to express our gratitude to the Swedish research funds, *The Bank of Sweden Tercentenary Foundation* and The *Swedish Research Council*, for their financial support; without their assistance this work would never have been possible.

Most importantly we want to thank our families for their unconditional support and encouragement.

Harold G. Nelson Erik Stolterman
Seattle   Djäkneböle

PRELUDE

Genesis is ongoing. As human beings, we continuously create things that help form the basis of the world as we know it. When we create these new things—tools, organizations, processes, symbols and systems—we engage in design. To come up with an idea, and to give form, structure and function to that idea, is at the core of design as a human activity. This book is about that activity.

Design is such a natural human ability that almost everyone is designing most of the time—whether they are conscious of it, or not. Framing our understanding in this way, we will use the concept of design to define, and promote, a new philosophical tradition; a new culture of inquiry and action. That tradition is identified here as *The Design Way*—the first tradition. This designerly approach applies to an infinite variety of design domains; including those fields that are traditionally thought of when we consider design, such as architectural or interior design, industrial design, engineering design, graphic design, urban design, information systems design, software design, fashion design and other forms of physical design. But our definition also allows us to encompass other design areas, such as organizational design, social systems design, educational systems design, work place design and healthcare design. Such a design approach can even be

1

applied to significant social institutions such as governments, including the design of democratic constitutions (Sunstein, 2001).

In our struggle to understand an ever more complex reality, we believe the current traditions of inquiry and action prevalent in our society do not give us the support we need—as leaders and designers—to meet the emergent challenges that now confront us. The world is changing rapidly, sometimes with intent, but too often by accident. The world has proven to be unpredictable, despite the best attempts of science and technology to bring predictability and control to worldly affairs. The laws of nature may be fixed, but the complex interactions of everyday events, whether provoked by accident or fate, result in unpredictable outcomes. The one thing that makes this state of affairs tolerable is the inchoate knowledge that change—desired change—can be wrought by human intention. Human intention, made visible and concrete through the instrumentality of design, enables us to create conditions, or artifacts, that facilitate the unfolding of human potential through *designed evolution* in contrast to an evolution based on chance and necessity—a highly unpredictable process.

In our attempts to design the world to be what we would like it to be, we find that the traditions at hand cannot fully support that task. Science, art, spirituality, economics and technology are all important traditions of inquiry. However, they do not embody the unique specifics of the design tradition, with its corresponding philosophy and praxis. Each of the prevailing traditions has developed a depth of knowledge and insight that is impressive, but it is often focused on a narrow aspect of our human experience—one that is necessary but not solely sufficient in the management of human affairs.

We believe the culture of inquiry and action that infuses design thinking is an essential part of the palette of human traditions. We are

2

not the only ones who think so. Other scholars (Cross, 2001) have investigated the concept of a design *tradition*. Yet, design has remained surprisingly invisible and unrecognized. This book is an attempt to change this by recognizing design as its own tradition and formulating its fundamental core of ideas. *The Design Way* does not present a ready-made recipe on how to engage in design. This is not a book about design praxis, which deserves several books of its own. It is not something exclusive to professional designers. It is a way to approach reality that intentionally embraces its vast richness and complexity.

Our ultimate desire is to encourage and promote a design *culture*. Now, what do we mean by this? For any tradition to flourish, that tradition requires a nurturing environment, a protective container within which its frontiers and prospects are defined and protected. A design tradition requires the enabling presence of a design culture, one that defines conceptual expanses and boundaries, and provides a context for setting particular limits on any design project. Such a design culture acts as a catalyst in the formation of social crucibles essential for sustaining the intensity of design action. It is a protective environment that provides the space and freedom necessary to foster a process that is both powerful and vulnerable at the same time.

What is presented in this book is a *composition* of what we believe a broad and deep understanding of design—and designing as a tradition of inquiry and action—should include. This composition is, in itself, a design. It is not an attempt to present a true or accurate description of an idealized design culture. Nor, is it an attempt to answer all questions that might emerge concerning what a design culture might, or ought to, be. It is our understanding of design, as its own tradition and not merely a variant of science, or art, or technology, or spirituality. It is an effort to build a deeper understanding of design,

3

based on ideas we believe must be present in the development and implementation of a design culture—the necessary ingredients for the release of design's full potential and promise for generative human agency.

The Design Way is an introduction to many ideas that deserve a book of their own. We feel that it is important, however, to present them here as a whole, as part of our composition. We are not proposing a particular theory, or a set of theorems, or axioms. Instead, we have chosen to use *foundations*, *fundamentals* and *metaphysics* as the unifying elements of the book. The foundations are equivalent to the first principles or causes of other traditions such as science. The fundamentals are identified as those core concepts of the design approach that can be learned and improved on through practice. The metaphysical issues arise as a consequence of the interaction of the foundations and fundamentals of the design tradition, with one another and with the larger domains of human existence.

This structure of foundations, fundamentals and metaphysics best reflects the level of our intention in making a case for a design culture. Over the years, we have found that there are emergent patterns informing the composition of our ideas as a whole. We find that it is possible to make a composition from this tripartite relationship; one that reflects, in different ways, what we see as the core of a design approach—a design way.

The idea of a design culture is one that promotes an understanding of design as transcendent of particular contexts, specific disciplines, or single concepts. For instance, it is commonly believed that design is simply a form of creativity. Creativity is thought of as the activity that gives design its special qualities. But, even though creativity is seminal to design—design is larger and more comprehensive. Design is

4

inclusive not only of creative thinking but includes innovative activity as well. Innovation differs from creativity in that innovation is action oriented. It is achieved through the manifestation and integration of creative concepts into the real world. Design is also a compound of rational, ideal and pragmatic inquiry. Design is constituted of reflective thinking, productive action and responsible follow through. Therefore, a single concept, such as creativity, does not capture the full richness of the design tradition.

A design culture needs to be broad in its scope and deep in its meaning and utility. Thinking about design in this way, we hope to define a firm platform from which designers, in any field, can bring this new appreciation for the potential of design into action. With this in mind, we will often use the term 'design' to stand for this broader meaning of a design culture.

The process of design is always the most effective and efficient means of getting organizations and individuals to new places. Design is therefore about leadership—and leadership is therefore an essential element of any design culture. Leadership today demands action and the ability to act, based on an overwhelming amount of insufficient information within restrictive limits of resources and time. These demands cannot be met solely from within the traditions of science, art, or pragmatic technology. These demands require leaders to imagine and implement adequate responses that are sustainable—in all their implications. This is a task that calls for judgment—not problem solving. It calls for *good* compositions—not *true* solutions. We argue that *The Design Way* is not only for designers, but for leaders as well. We believe that leaders and designers are often one and the same, and that it is important for leaders to recognize their challenge as that of a designer—to find direction and destination via the design tradition.

5

The Design Way is based on the notion of *reflections* and *substance*. We hope that the book, as a composition, will evoke an understanding of *what design is all about*. Each chapter is an attempt to reflect that substance. Each reflection reveals only one image, which is not enough by itself. It is hoped that, by moving among different reflections, recognition and understanding of the substance itself (i.e., what design is all about) will emerge. This means we encourage readers to choose to read the reflections (or chapters) that seem most interesting or suitable to them. Even if the book is designed as a composition with an overarching structure, it is possible to read the chapters independently. For example, many readers have found it more beneficial to read the *Systems* chapter after reading most of the other chapters because of its dissimilar tone and more methodological approach to content.

Our hope is that each reflection or image of design will intrigue the reader to delve further, eventually creating a more comprehensive understanding of the substance of design. This is also true of the individual graphics found throughout the text. The graphics are meant to not merely illustrate the text, as the text is not meant to just explain the graphics. The graphics in many cases are meant to momentarily arrest the progress of the *acquiring eye* in order to give the *reflective eye* time and space to provoke questions and elicit understandings that are relevant to the reader's *own* experiences and understanding. In this way our ideas can start to become the reader's ideas.

We also hope, that through reading it, *The Design Way* will sway others to participate in the creation of a design culture as a consequence of the influences of a revitalized and reconstituted tradition of design. This means the book is not just for designers, or those who hope to become designers, but for everyone. Each person, in his or her own way, can become responsible for the creation of a design culture. With such a design culture in place, designers will find themselves being encouraged to safely pursue their design intentions in an open and supportive environment.

In our attempts to present a broad understanding of design, we have been pragmatic in our relation to other sources. We have drawn from many intellectual traditions, and we have used philosophers and design thinkers in ways not always obvious from a standard perspective. When we make a reference to a specific philosopher, or thinker, this does not imply that we endorse the entirety of his or her work.

To make the design tradition visibly distinct from other intellectual traditions, we sometimes portray those traditions in ways that may not do them full justice. To make these traditions visible, we might use an idealized and sometimes simplified understanding of their essential nature. This may seem offensive to some readers, who are led to believe our purpose is to diminish the richness of the other traditions in order to make the design tradition appear more valuable. This is not our intention, however, but merely an artifact of our pedagogical approach.

When it comes to our own ideas, we have tried to be congruent with the design tradition. It is the composition of our thoughts—as a whole—that carries the primary message. This means that when we discuss specific concepts, such as judgment, composition, contracting, communication, or character, we do this from within the design tradition. We do not try to provide universal definitions of these concepts that would apply across other traditions of inquiry and action. They are defined through use in pragmatic design ways, with the specific purpose of revealing our grasp of design as a whole.

I. THE FIRST TRADITION

Humans did not discover fire—they designed it. The wheel was not something our ancestors merely stumbled over in a stroke of good luck; it, too, was designed. The habit of labeling significant human achievements as 'discoveries', rather than 'designs', discloses a critical bias in our Western tradition. Absent from the conflicting descriptions of Leonardo da Vinci, as either scientist or artist, is the missing insight into his essential nature as a designer. His practical, purpose-driven and integrative approach to the world—an archetypal designer's approach—is primarily what made him so distinct in his own time, as well as our own. Through his imaginative genius, augmentations to the real world were made manifest. This has been the contribution of all designers throughout human history. Outside of nature, they are the prime creators of our experienced reality.

Carefully designed artifacts accompany the remains of our earliest ancestors. Designed implements have been found which predate the earliest human fossil remains discovered so far. In fact, it is evidence of design ability, and activity, which allows an archeologist to distinguish between a species that is not quite human and one that is. So, it appears that it is our very ability to design which determines our humanness.

Design is the ability to imagine *that-which-does-not-yet-exist*, to make it appear in concrete form as a new, purposeful addition to the real world. *Design is the first tradition* among the many traditions of inquiry and action developed over time, including art, religion, science and technology. We design our cosmologies, our homes, our businesses and our lives, as well as our material artifacts. As such, design touches nearly every aspect of our experienced world. It is an important capacity, not only for those who wish to be designers, but also for those who are served in the design relationship as well. Things that really count, and are highly valued, come from design, when not directly from nature.

Possessing the ability to engage so powerfully in the world is the essence of human potential. But, it is also true that humans are fallible. Design activities can do and have done great service for humanity. But design has done great harm as well. We cannot know for certain, that what we design is what ought to be designed. We cannot know what the unintended consequences of a design will be, and we cannot know, ahead of time, the full, systemic effects of a design implementation. We can be god-like in the co-creation of the world, yet we cannot be god-like in our guarantee that the design will be only what we intended it to be, for the reasons we intended, and with a full understanding of the necessity of the design in the first place. We will always be startled by the appearance of unintended consequences and other unpleasant surprises.

An archetypal designer is represented in the Greek pantheon of gods in the persona of Hephaistos—the lame god. Hephaistos' counterparts appear in African and Middle Eastern mythology as well. Depending on the particular story you read, the reasons for Hephaistos' lameness vary. However, as a consequence of his

10

condition, he was required to create tools and devices (artifacts, if you will) which enabled him to overcome his handicap, setting him apart from the other, more perfect gods. His great creativity and craftsmanship attracted the attention of the other gods, who contracted for his services in the creation of jewelry, homes, armor and other godly necessities.

Hephaistos had the full potential of the other gods, but did not have their full capacity. This lack of capacity required him to bring things into existence in order to overcome his imperfection. With the aid of his own creations, he became the archetypal designer in order to fulfill his potential. In the process, he began to improve the experienced realities of the other, uncompromised deities. Human designers share Hephaistos' challenge. We must design, because we are not perfect. Yet, even though we lack this capacity for perfection, we share the potential of our creator gods to do great good, or immense harm, as we have continually demonstrated to others and ourselves since the dawn of civilization.

As shown in the figures below, the question of why we design does not lend itself to a simple answer (see Fig. I-1). Like Hephaistos, we have to design because we want to survive, but humans also seem to have a will for continuous improvement and development. Different psychological theories also tell us that we have other purposes; for instance, we want to make a difference in the world. At the highest level, it might be that we want to participate in *the* creation. In effect, we want to make the world *our* world.

We also display varying levels of motivation (see Fig. I-2). At the most basic level, we as human beings are compelled to design—it is our calling as agents of free will, who through design intelligence, can

11

- Survive
- IMPROVE
- DEVELOP
- THRIVE
- EVOLVE
- SERVE OTHERS
- MAKE SOMETHING OF LASTING QUALITY
- CREATE SOMETHING OF REAL CONSEQUENCE
- PARTICIPATE IN THE NEVER-ENDING GENESIS

Fig. I-1 Purpose of Designing

act with *design will*. As humans with design will, we are impelled to create new meaning, new forms and new realities. The source of our free will and the compelling nature of our design remain a mystery of human nature. Joseph Campbell's (1968) description of the 'hero's quest', a common theme in most mythologies, begins with the 'call' for a hero or heroine to step out of his/her normal and comfortable life into a dangerous but necessary quest for life enhancing wisdom. The call can be ignored, but not without consequences. The call, when answered, initiates a process leading to a life-affirming boon for society—motivated by the desire to be in service to others. But, that is not our only motivator, we also have the desire to be in more control of as much of our lives as possible.

On a more abstract level, we are drawn to design because we may feel a lack of wholeness—we do not find the world in a condition that is satisfying or fulfilling for us. And, ultimately, we are motivated to design because it is an accessible means to enlightenment, to bring

12

order, and to give meaning to our lives. It is a way for us, as it was for Hephaistos, to become what we are capable of being, but do not have the full capacity to be, without our creations to aid us (what Sigmund Freud called being "prosthetic gods").

- TO CONTROL
- FROM NECESSITY
- BRING ORDER
- GIVE MEANING
- CALLING—DESIGN WILL
- FOR ENLIGHTENMENT / WISDOM
- LACK OF WHOLENESS
- TO BE OF SERVICE

Fig. I-2 Motivation for Designing

Design, as a unique way of thinking and acting, does not have a long, well-developed scholarly history. Other intellectual traditions, such as science and art, have enjoyed thousands of years of considered thought. But, in the Western tradition at the time of Socrates, Plato and Aristotle, design, as a focus of philosophic reflection, was divided. The word philosophy is a compound word composed of two Greek root terms: *philo* and *sophia*. Philo is love and sophia is wisdom; thus the term philosophy means the love of wisdom. During the pre-Socratic period in Greece, the defined understanding of wisdom or sophia, was the *knowing hand*. Sophia was an integration of thinking and action, as well as reflection and production.

13

However, during the time of the above-mentioned philosophers, sophia was divided. In the philosophic writings of Aristotle, wisdom (sophia), became primarily the concern for first principles and causes—thus cleaving it from practical wisdom and productive action. Sophia was further divided into knowledge of ideals and the capacity for practical actions.

Sophia was not only divided into separate parts, but the resulting components were placed at the extremes of a hierarchy. In Plato's Republic, those who *thought* about things were elevated to the pinnacle of society, while those who *made* things were positioned at the bottom of the social hierarchy. This hierarchy can be seen even in today's world. Polarities between people, such as white collar and blue-collar workers, management and labor, thinkers and doers, continue to play out this division in sophia. The split widens further in the polarization of ideas, like rigor versus relevance, feeling versus intellect, thinking versus doing, or abstract versus concrete.

Design's historical roots were further frayed when Aristotle's four causes—material cause (substance), instrumental cause (means), formal cause (forms), final cause (ends)—used to describe and explain the world, were reduced in the middle ages to just two causes: material cause and instrumental cause (i.e., pure science and applied science). The original understanding of design in the pre-Socratic era not only included Aristotle's full complement of causes, but required the addition of other causes that had their focus on making and production—in distinction to just description and explanation.

These historical polarizations and separations have influenced the way in which we today can understand, or justify taking any collective action. Without the tradition of design in place, in its pre-Socratic form, we have had to look to other traditions for insight into the nature and management of change.

The dominant trigger for initiating change in human affairs is, today, primarily based on the existence of a clear and immediate understanding of a particular problem or set of problems. Political action, professional performance, economic decisions, social planning and business choices are almost entirely justified on the grounds that life is a set of problems requiring practical, efficient and effective solutions. Much of formal education or training is based on preparing students to better identify and solve problems creatively, quickly, fairly, rationally and prudently. This essentially reactive mode, applied to every realm of life, is reinforced and supported by well-developed procedures for problem solving. Horst Rittel (1972) has identified such procedures as *tame problem solving procedures* (see Fig. I-3).

1. UNDERSTAND PROBLEM
2. GATHER INFORMATION
3. ANALYZE INFORMATION
4. GENERATE SOLUTIONS
5. ASSESS THE SOLUTIONS
6. IMPLEMENT
7. TEST
8. MODIFY

Fig. I-3 Solving Tame Problems (Rittel, 1972)

Tame problems are appropriate for simple or trivial concerns, but more important or significant issues are better characterized,

15

according to Rittel, as *wicked problems* (as shown in Fig. I-4). The characteristics of wicked problems do not lend themselves to simple procedures, or even easy characterizations. If taken seriously, the wicked nature of these problems can lead to paralysis. This paralysis is most often skirted by the assumption that most wicked problems can be recast as tame problems. This, of course, exacerbates the original wicked problem and creates an even greater mess.

- CANNOT BE EXHAUSTIVELY FORMULATED
- EVERY FORMULATION IS A STATEMENT OF A SOLUTION
- NO STOPPING RULE
- NO TRUE OR FALSE
- NO EXHAUSTIVE LIST OF OPERATIONS
- MANY EXPLANATIONS FOR THE SAME PROBLEM
- EVERY PROBLEM IS A SYMPTOM OF ANOTHER PROBLEM
- NO IMMEDIATE OR ULTIMATE TEST
- ONE-SHOT SOLUTIONS
- EVERY PROBLEM IS ESSENTIALLY UNIQUE
- PROBLEM SOLVER HAS NO RIGHT TO BE WRONG

Fig. I-4 Characteristics of Wicked Problems (Rittel, 1972)

The characteristics of a wicked problem listed above are not descriptive of a process for determining solutions to such problems, but are merely explanative of the nature of wicked problems. These characteristics are the result of the limits and paradoxes of reason when applied to real-world situations in human affairs that are unique, contingent, unpredictable and complex. (For a full description of these characteristics of wicked problems, please see Rittel's complete article.)

By treating a wicked problem as a tame problem, energy and resources are misdirected, resulting in solutions that are not only ineffective, but can actually create more difficulty; because the approach used is an intervention that is, by necessity, inappropriately conceptualized. Most of our significant everyday encounters with a problematic reality have the characteristics of wicked problems. Very few everyday situations of any importance can be appropriately and unerringly described as tame problems. For instance, there is never only one best solution to such problems. There are only solutions that are good or bad. There is no one correct approach or methodology for solving these problems, and it is not possible to formulate one comprehensive and accurate description of a problematic situation from the beginning. Tame and wicked problems are not governed by the same logic. The strategies developed to deal with tame problems are not just different in degree, but different in kind from those required for dealing with the complexity, ambiguity and epistemological uniqueness of wicked problems.

The focus on *problems*, whether wicked or tame, as the primary justifiable trigger for taking action in human affairs has limited our ability to frame change as an outcome of intention and purpose. It means that wise action, or wisdom, is starved of its potential (Nelson, 1994). Wisdom—specifically what we call design wisdom—is a much richer concept than problem solving, because it shifts one's thoughts from focusing only on avoiding undesirable states, to focusing on intentional actions that lead to states of reality which are desirable and appropriate.

As only the intellectual or reflective components of the pre-Socratic concept of wisdom (i.e., the wisdom of reason) remain present in Western thought, wisdom is most often treated as simply the summation of data, translated into information, which is then transformed into knowledge. On the rare occasions when wisdom is discussed in practical settings, the challenge is how to make and maintain the linkages between the rational components of wisdom, while accommodating the challenges of unique particular design situations.

The wisdom of the *knowing hand*, that of making, producing and acting, must be connected to the wisdom of reason. But, wisdom—in the realm of design—requires that we take a step back. Design wisdom requires the reconstitution of sophia. Design wisdom is an integration of reason with observation, reflection, imagination, action and production.

Another demand that design wisdom makes upon us is to reintroduce the *analog* into a world long dominated by the *digital* and the *analytic*. The digital and analytic perspectives have heavily influenced Western traditions of thought for centuries. For instance, the division of the day into hours, minutes and seconds that are indifferent to the particular qualities of any one day is an example of the digital. The division of land into grids indifferent to terrain or social habitation is another example of the digital. The division of sound or light waves into electronic pulses is another form of digital translation. The digital approach divides information into packets that are stable and congruent but detached from the qualities of the substance or event itself.

The division of all reality into disciplines of science is an example of the analytic. The analytic is an approach that divides things into constituent parts or categories of similarity. The division of human

18

service into areas of professional expertise is another example of the analytic. This has allowed us to make significant advances in technology and related scientific endeavors. Unfortunately, concurrent with this, the analog has become conspicuous in its absence in contemporary technical societies. This absence is a natural consequence of societies divided and separated by specialization, by taxonomies and categorizations, by social hierarchies and by administrative conveniences.

Individuals struggle to comprehend their experience of life as an analog reality—an integrated, complex whole, without clear, distinct and separate taxonomies or categories. The digital and analytic approach to making sense of this undifferentiated experience helps to facilitate intentional change by reducing the overwhelming complexity of any particular situation and by providing instrumental distinctions that can become elements in new design compositions. Design wisdom has the ability to shift from an analog experience of life, to a digital or analytic perspective of the world and *back again*. This is done by means of a design process that begins initially with a complex, undifferentiated situation, which then transitions through a process of discernment and distinction and ultimately terminates with the integration of innovative designs into a desired seamless reality for those being served directly or affected incidentally. Therefore, one of the most vital aspects of design is that the outcome of any necessary digital and analytic intervention must be transformed back into the analog. This is to assure that, with each new design addition, life continues to be experienced as a whole.

One more component of design wisdom concerns the nature of *change*. Change is an oft-evoked concept in politics, planning, management and other forms of intervention, but it is often not clearly articulated. In the tradition of scientific thinking, change is a consequence of either *chance* or *necessity*. Probability theory and statistical analysis are examples of our approach to change, as a result of chance. In human affairs, chance is often experienced as luck, or fate, whereas scientific principles, or laws, and rules of behavior are examples of how we react when necessity (or certainty) is the cause of change.

Design wisdom—as a first tradition—provides an escape from this limited state of affairs. Change, as a consequence of *design cause* or *intention*, is an approach available to us, as a third option (Nelson, 1987). In order to develop a tradition of design thinking, this concept of *intention* needs to be added as an agent of change to the ones already existing. The concept of change needs to be deepened as well in this context. Change—in relationship to design wisdom—has multiple levels of meaning, significance and consequence, as shown in Fig. I-5.

CHANGE
IS
DIFFERENCE
•
CHANGE OF DIFFERENCE
IS
PROCESS
•
CHANGE OF PROCESS
IS
EVOLUTION
•
CHANGE OF EVOLUTION
IS
DESIGN

Fig. I-5 Hierarchy of Change

The challenge to cultures, or societies, on how to deal with change at these multiple levels was formulated by Arnold J. Toynbee (1948), and presented in mythic terms in the work of Joseph Campbell (1968)(see Fig. I-6). According to Toynbee's findings, based on his research into the behavior of past civilizations, social systems historically evoke four types of responses when confronted by change. The only cultures that successfully move through major challenges, or crises, are those that engage in change in a manner that is consistent with design wisdom and leads to transformational change.

Of course, cultures, civilizations, nations and other forms of large-scale social systems can escape major change over extended periods of time. But, when the pressures for change build internally, or externally, accidentally or intentionally, successful survival and improvement seem to come only as consequences of an approach that can radically transform the existing order of things as per Toynbee's model. Such an approach can be characterized as a design approach.

A. "RETURN" TO THE GOOD OLD DAYS

B. "HANG-ON-TO" THE PRESENT

C. "REACH" FOR A UTOPIA

D. RADICALLY "TRANSFORM" THE EXISTING

Fig. I-6 Toynbee's Social Change Strategies

Change is a vital part of our experience of life. We often feel pushed into design because of the perceived pace of change in contemporary human affairs. We are pushed again by the explosion of information we are challenged to gather, understand and utilize. We are pushed still further by the immense increase in Western technologic development, with its fallout of incomprehensible numbers of distinct tools, machines, products and all manner of designed artifacts. Thus, we are confronted with more varieties of *what can be done*, than with *what we know we want done*.

But, it is also true, that we are pulled into design because it allows us to initiate intentional action out of strength, hope, passion, desire and love. It is action that generates more energy than it consumes. It is innovative inquiry that creates more resources—of greater variety and potential—than are used. Design action is distinct from problem action, which is initiated out of need, fear, weakness, hate, pain and other reactive motivations.

A desire for change is often assumed to imply a need for comprehensive analysis, and rational decision-making, leading to a clear choice for action. The reality is that analysis often leads to ever-greater numbers of paths, which then require more analysis. The consequence is that decisions cannot, and are not, made rationally—at least not in the rational tradition of scientific comprehensiveness. The real world is much too complex to be understood comprehensively.

Design—as an alternative to this rational approach—utilizes a process of *composition*, which pulls a variety of elements into relationship with one another, forming a functional assembly that can serve the purposes, and intentions, of diverse populations of human beings. For example, any human activity system is an example of this, including transportation systems, governance systems, economics systems, health systems and education systems. Whenever such systems are created or modified as designs, a compositional approach is used. We also utilize the same process when we create new material goods and services. In addition, the composition process creates emergent

22

qualities that become apparent when these designs are viewed as wholes. These **emergent qualities** transcend a design's functional qualities, often serving deeper, more significant, needs and desires.

So, to summarize a bit, the design tradition's thread of continuity frayed, and finally broke, over the centuries, as the Western world poured its focus and resources on the development of science and technology. Yet, to be able to successfully deal with change in the 21st Century, it is now critical that we pick up those frayed design threads, and weave them into new patterns, integrating their wisdom into a more holistic fabric of life.

How do we go about this? We believe that for a design tradition to flourish, we will need to create a design culture. That is, a culture which embraces a social, economic, political and personal environment into which designing, and designers, are not only invited, but welcomed. It is equally important to populate this culture with competent designers who have the education, experience and desire to practice design from a broader perspective than the traditional practices of material design.

Why is there—at this point in time—such a need for a design culture? And, is it possible to present some essential qualities of such a culture in a book? We believe that it is, and this book is just such an attempt. Of course, an entire culture can never be created by merely writing a book, but we hope to initiate a reflective dialogue on what a design culture might look like—at least in the beginning stages of its development, joining with others with similar interests, such as Bela H. Banathy (1996).

It's our thought that the first step in establishing a design culture is to conceptualize design as a unique way of looking at the human condition. To that end, we need to develop and use design wisdom as

23

a frame of reference grounded in its own unique tradition. It is, in effect, our first tradition, as was discussed at the beginning of the book. The remainder of this book deals with considering the character and consequences of this idea more fully.

In every particular design, there are specific dimensions of art, technology and science, but in the totality of that design, in its inclusiveness of generalized aspects of the experienced world, it has a commonality with all applications of design. Herbert Simon (1969), speaking from an engineering background, made a seminal contribution to the development of a broader understanding of design by introducing the concept of the science of the artificial—design. The continuation and expansion of this idea, in more recent work, is collected in Margolin and Buchanan (1995), and in Buchanan and Margolin (1995).

That design thinkers hail from a variety of backgrounds should not come as a surprise. Designers from any design field, formally defined or not, can relate to other designers because they all are striving towards the same goal; they are hoping to add to, or change, the real world. They do this through their creativity, and innovation, in both particular, and universal, ways.

A culture is never a natural occurrence. A culture is always created by design. Cultures are a living tension between tradition and innovation, between stability and change. This type of social structure and process (i.e., culture), can always be changed, developed, deepened, misunderstood, or misinterpreted. As we work to develop a conscious design tradition, we must remember that any change in cultural tradition can easily be blocked by habits we do not see, or understand. A culture often consists of ideas, guidelines and a 'common sense' understanding that we take for granted, often without questioning

24

their origin or benefit. This means that there is a need for both open and critical minds in the creation of a design culture.

Even when we focus on the cultural similarities among different kinds of designers, we do so based on a recognition and acceptance of their differences. It is important to acknowledge that every formally recognized professional designer has a specific *field of design expertise*—a range of specific crafts, skills and knowledge, such as: industrial design, architecture, information design, software design, urban design, organizational design, educational design, instructional design, etc. It is even more important to emphasize that every informally recognized designer has a similar field of expertise. It goes without saying that every designer needs knowledge and skills, concerning materials, tools, methods, languages, traditions, styles, etc., in his or her specific field.

This book is not about those focused skills. Instead it is about the cultural tradition within which the designer acts. We argue that, to be a thoughtful and responsible designer, any general understanding of what design is ultimately about has to be challenged and critically analyzed, by you—the individual designer, client, stakeholder—or anyone else affected by design. In addition, any understanding of design should be the result of reflective practice, intellectual apperception and intentional choice. This book is meant to be a resource in the creation of such an individual understanding of design.

25

II. FOUNDATIONS

Although it is common to assume that any new way of thinking must be defined by a new paradigm (Kuhn, 1962), it is equally important to uncover the conceptual foundations upon which a new culture of inquiry plans to stand. The design hypostasis we present in the following four chapters acts as the supporting platform for the design approach.

We believe these chapters cover the seminal ideas supportive of a design culture. When studied, these foundational concepts will help any designer—or champion of design—develop an understanding of the conditions necessary for real design inquiry and action to flourish.

In these chapters, we will focus on *the real, service, systems* and *the whole,* and explore each of these foundational precepts in detail.

1. THE REAL

We noted at the beginning of *The First Tradition* that scientists tend to label ancient human designs, such as fire or the wheel, as 'discoveries'. This penchant is an extension of the traditional approach for labeling scientific phenomena. When a researcher first becomes aware of something in the physical realm—something which has existed since time immemorial, but which has just now come to this researcher's consciousness—he or she is said to have 'discovered' that phenomena. We accept that scientists have 'discovered' gravity, evolution, entropy and other seminal natural laws, through careful observation and critical evaluation—revealing that which is *true*. But in design, we are additionally interested in that which is *ideal* and that which is *real*.

In the theoretical world of science, we do not think about natural laws or truths as being designed. But, in the *real* world—the present environment that surrounds all of us—we understand that we 'create' as well as 'discover' reality. This is because the real world, which is essentially an artificial world, is very much a created design.

We do not talk about our cities as if they were strange findings that popped up out of nowhere, or about our cars and houses as 'discoveries', or about our social organizations as 'natural artifacts' suddenly brought to light by careful empiricism. We see them as created. We see them as true, in the sense that they exist. We do not see them as true, in the same way a scientific law is true. They are not, deterministically, the only possible and necessary car, house, or organization. Nor are they great accidents of time and chance.

We know, in our experience of everyday life, that we have the power to decide what will become a part of our real world. We can design the real world in almost any form imaginable. And, we are quite certain that there is little chance of some day discovering the 'right' answers to the question of what kind of world we ought to have created. Although there are people who claim they have access to the truth—i.e., that they are able to discern what should, or should not, be regarded as an appropriate addition to our real world—most of us know that the way the world is designed is a result of a series of human judgments. We understand that we ought to do the best we can to create a world of quality, beauty and fulfillment—we're also aware that not everyone will use the power of design for these same ends.

There are basic truths that, in many ways, help us to make these judgments. For example, we know, nowadays, about the fragility of our natural environment. We understand the importance of being concerned about water and air. Almost all of us are convinced (this may not be a truth yet, but only a hope) that we have to take care of all forms of life on the planet, if we want our own species to survive. We have learned how to make products that are safer for ourselves and the environment. Unfortunately, to integrate all of these understandings into a single design situation is often too complex a task for us. No matter how much we want to satisfy all possible truths, in a design situation, we will find that some of them are contradictory, unclear, or not yet fully revealed. We will find that these truths do not provide us with one single correct choice.

This means we will never be able to ground design on the idea that the 'right' design is out there, embedded in reality and just itching to be discovered. To the contrary, design will always be about creating something that does not yet exist. It is not about finding something already in existence. Science can help us in our design process by providing knowledge about structures, laws and processes that reveal the natural world. But the primary thing this kind of knowledge gives us is a description, or explanation, of already existing things. Science cannot provide insight into what *should* be brought into existence, through intention, imagination and innovation. It can only assist.

Designers want to be able to make good design judgments that will, at the very least, make a company efficient, a nonprofit effective, or a governmental agency politically popular. They want to make designs that lead to better products, services, organizational behavior, or global sustainability. They also want to be seen as designers worth the compensation, prestige and trust they desire, or receive.

Leaders and managers, as well, are facing ever-increasing demands on their design judgment skills. The market overflows with workshops, and training sessions, that promise to provide the right sequence of experiences that leads to painless, accessible and cost-effective problem solving skills. The underlying promise being that these skills will consistently provide ready-made, transferable solutions to the complex problems facing leaders today.

A desire for consistency and certainty has been part of the human condition for as long as recorded time. The earliest cosmologies, with their associated rites and rituals, were all meant to give structure to chaos and mystery. But, even with a cosmology in place, there has always been less predictability than desired, and more unpredictability than tolerable. Ancient Greek decision-makers would go to great

31

effort to ask the Oracle at Delphi for a simple answer to their straight-forward question, only to be given responses that, by necessity, required deeper thinking on the questioner's side. The early Christians found that their leader spoke only in parables, leaving centuries of interpretation as to what the 'true' answers were. Despite the popularity of these traditional sources of wisdom, decision-makers have continued to look for other means of inquiry that will provide information that is more accessible, straightforward, accurate and consistent over time.

In the Western tradition, the right answer was soon identified as an outcome of rational thought, using the protocol of scientific method. This approach worked so well for gaining a better under-standing of the natural world, and for the creation of sophisticated technology, that it was only natural that managers, administrators, and even designers, would begin to depend heavily on this particular form of inquiry as well.

However, this scientific approach, with some exceptions, has not provided the kind of guarantee of outcomes one would imagine possible. This comes from confusion between what is *true*, and what is *real*. Science deals only with what is true, but managers—and definitely designers—must deal with what is real, in addition to what is true.

When something is true, it has to be true in all cases and situations. A statement that is sometimes true, and sometimes not, is not what we accept as a scientific truth. Science deals with what is general and uni-versal. There are extensive discussions concerning whether some of the newer scientific methods used in social science, such as case studies, interpretative studies, or qualitative methods, have the ability to create any kind of universal, or generalizable, truths. If a rational method leads only to an understanding of a specific case, and not to some universal truth, then it is not really considered to be a scientific method. Based on this kind of thinking, modern social science is often accused by other researchers of being the same thing as journalism or even creative writing.

In science, we strive to infer from specific particulars, to the universal. This is done by the method of induction. Through science, we can also explain something quite particular with the help of the universal, by the method of deduction. But, the process for creating the *ultimate particular* (see Fig. 1-1) is not based on scientific induction or scientific deduction. There is no scientific approach to determining the particular because science is a process of discerning abstractions that apply across categories or taxonomies of phenomena, while the particular is singular and unique. Creating that which is unique and thus particular, therefore, cannot be accomplished using a scientific approach. An action taken by an individual at a specific time and place is an example of something that is an ultimate particular.

The outcome of a specific design process, such as a car, a curriculum, or an organizational structure, is an ultimate particular. It is something unique. It is not the universal car, the universal organizational structure, or curriculum. We are creating a particular, which, when taken together with other particulars, makes up the whole of our experienced reality. Even when products are designed in great numbers, with wide distribution, they still have the quality of being particular and not universal, since they do not represent the only possibility for accomplishing the same end or serving the same purpose.

Design is a process of moving from the particular, general and universal to the *ultimate particular*—the specific design (a related concept called *full particular* is developed in Sunstein, 2001). The way

33

we do this is by making design judgments. What we desire to come into existence is a matter of judgment—based on design *will* (volition) and *intention* (aim)—and can never be found in explanation, description, or prediction. (The concept of judgment as related to design is developed more fully in the *Judgment* chapter.) Design will and design intentions are the means for initiating and directing change based on human agency. It is design will and design intention, guided by design judgment, that transforms the abstractness of relevant scientific knowledge into a final unique design, the ultimate particular. The ultimate particular is that which is manifested in the world.

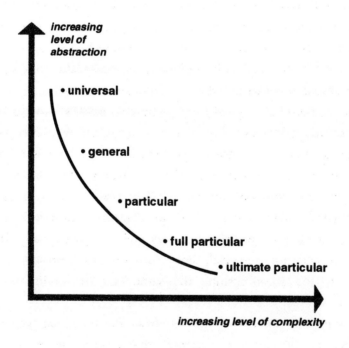

Fig. 1-1 Universal to Ultimate Particular

In design, we are not dealing with a universal truth—we are dealing with the particular; as well as with that which is real. Distinctions between what is true (e.g., universal or general) and what is real (e.g., particular, full particular and ultimate particular) can be made in the following ways. A painting by Cézanne is real; the atomic weight of copper is true. An experience is real; a scientific observation is true. An organization is real; a proven fact is true. An individual's perspective is real; a predictable event is true. The true comes from accurate descriptions, and explanations, through controlled observation, such as William James's "tough-minded" empiricism. The true can also come from careful abstract reasoning, and logic; as in William James's "tender-minded" rationalism (James, 1975). The real, on the other hand, is a result of action, taken through judgment, and formed by intention. Even if this distinction between the true and the real can be challenged from a purely philosophical perspective, it is valid and vital from the perspective of design.

Right decisions and appropriate actions in human activities do not and cannot arise from what is true only. When this fact is not appreciated, it leads both designers and decision-makers into dead-end states of analysis paralysis and value paralysis. Decisions, and actions, must be based on what is real, in addition to what is true. The real and the true are, of course, not exclusive. When dealing with the real, we often benefit from the kind of support given to us by the true. Scientific knowledge is essential to any designer. But knowing about the true is not enough when dealing with the real, and the ultimate particular. There should be symmetry between the real and the true, not polarity. We need to find unity between the two, rather than compromise.

Over time, many different ways of engaging in inquiry have been designed (Churchman, 1971) as opposed to being discovered or

imposed by nature. These differing forms of inquiry have been sufficiently successful—in the right context, and at certain moments in
history—as to be championed as 'superior' forms of inquiry, regardless of the situation or need. This is especially true of inquiry styles
that focus on revealing truth. The hegemony of science and scientific
thought, in the developed world over the last century, is an indicator
of the winner of the most recent battle for dominance among systems
of inquiry. A belief in the scientific method, as the only valid method
of inquiry for describing and explaining the world, is a hallmark of our
technologic age. Science, as an activity of disciplined inquiry, has often
been called the new religion of the contemporary age.

The design tradition, however, demands that we follow a different
path. The choice a designer makes, as to how to acquire knowledge,
deeply affects how his or her design work is done. If the designer
chooses a scientific approach, the whole design process will have
strong similarities to the research process. This will influence not only
what is considered to be a precondition of the design, but also what is
possible, what is needed, what is desired and what the eventual outcome will be.

C. West Churchman introduced the idea of designing systems of
rational inquiry by contrasting, and comparing, historical forms of
inquiry. The basic types of rational inquiry Churchman discussed are:
fact nets, consensus, representation, dialectic, progress, mechanism,
teleology and probability. Churchman used the thought processes of
famous philosophers as examples of the designs of inquiry he
presented. All the approaches he discussed are constructed in the
tradition of the true—the scientific search for knowledge. They are all
based on the idea of a rational approach that is guided by strict rules
on how to go about finding knowledge. In today's world of design, we

36

can find modern approaches resembling all of these various scientific traditions. A designer can greatly benefit from having a basic knowledge of traditional systems of inquiry. Such knowledge can help in evaluating the constant flow of 'new' approaches.

These approaches however, are not the only ones that can influence how a society and its designers acquire knowledge. In some cultures, the most dominant form of inquiry is the *spiritual*. In the spiritual tradition, knowledge is not necessarily something we have to gain for ourselves, or discover in the world. It is instead handed down to us, through different channels, from some kind of divine or spiritual source. The work of a designer, who builds on this tradition, will be radically different from designs based on scientific methods of inquiry. It is not uncommon, even in today's technologic world, to find designs inspired by and even argued, to be 'given' to humans from a higher source.

Another form of inquiry, over which there is a great deal of disagreement, is defined as *intuition*. Intuition is a form of unconscious knowing. A basic version of intuition is *instinct*. When we find animals engaging in design-like activity (creating tools for instance) we do not ascribe any advanced forms of inquiry to their behavior. Instead, we define their behavior as instinctive and not based on reflective reasoning at all. In the same way, it is possible to understand some of our human design behaviors as more a result of instinct, rather than reason and reflection. At a much higher level, intuition is an unconscious knowing gained through a unification of complex sense data, resulting in an integrated understanding of real-time experience.

There are many types of relationships that develop between these varying forms of inquiry. Most often, the relationship is defined as either a polarity or a continuum. One of the more enduring relationships is the polarity that exists between the two cultures of inquiry identified by C. P. Snow (1959); that of science and the humanities. An equally enduring example of a continuum relationship is that defined between art and science. On this continuum, for example, architecture has been placed at the midpoint. In similar fashion, design of any type is often defined as occurring at the same midpoint. Design is also considered to be at a midpoint between intuition and logic, or imagination and reason. Every chosen form of inquiry—intuitive, artistic, scientific, logic, or composite thereof—will lead to a specific body of knowledge. The chosen form of inquiry influences both what constitutes knowledge and how knowledge is gained. Each particular approach is based on some fundamental assumptions concerning what it means to create knowledge.

We suggest that design, as presented in *The Design Way*, is based on a compound form of inquiry, composed of *true, ideal* and *real* approaches to gaining knowledge (see Fig. 1-2). As we've said, there is a broad spectrum of inquiry systems that have been designed over the course of human history. Some are long forgotten, while others still form the skeleton upon which we base particular ways of asking, and answering, questions. Questions ultimately intended to expose the essence of the human condition. In our contemporary world, there are several common forms of inquiry in use at any one time.

Among these is the *ideal*. The notion of the ideal refers to the kind of inquiry devoted to the realm of norms and values. It is focused on knowledge that says something about how the world 'ought' to be in respect to some higher order, spiritual constitution, or idealistic system.

Inquiry into what is *true* is the most common form of inquiry and is associated with artistic and religious thinking as much as it is with

38

scientific thinking. Inquiry into the true, and inquiry into the ideal, are well-formed modalities with long traditions of development, suitable vocabularies, historically defined frames of reference and well-known instruments of thought. For example, the scientific method has been used for determination of the true. Enlightenment, through reflection, contemplation, meditation, or prayer, has been used to access the ideal. The same historical development has not occurred in the case of inquiry into the real, and there is no time-tested body of knowledge to count on as a consequence.

designs of inquiry	outcomes
real	particulars
true	facts
ideal	norms

Fig. 1-2 Components of Design Inquiry

Inquiry into the real is not only a form of reflective, abstract, or conceptual inquiry, but it is also action-oriented. Its focus, when used for design purposes, is on production and innovation. The real, as a focus of inquiry, is essential to the ultimate design goal of creating the *not-yet-existing*. It is about helping to operationalize the creation of the *not-yet-real* and the particular as defined earlier.

Designs of Inquiry & Action

foundations	the real	the true	the ideal
intention	evoke the particular	reason the universal or general	reveal the ultimate
purpose	serve & fulfill	understand	transcend
form	systemic	taxonomic	natural or ordained
unity	wholeness	comprehensive	oneness
fundamentals			
motivation	desiderata & inspiration	curiosity & wonder	angst & awe
understanding	meaning	fact	enlightenment
input	imagination	observation	inspiration
meaning making	judgment	reason & logic	meditation
output	composition	description & explanation	perfection
process	creation & production	knowing	being

Fig. 1-3 Designs of Inquiry: The Real, True and Ideal

When we compare the three forms of inquiry, the real, the true and the ideal, some immediate differences and similarities are revealed (see Fig. 1-3). We will not go through this comparison in detail here (since it is covered in detail in the following chapters). We will just mention that using an integrative model, like the one above, is a good way to reflect on, and build a deeper appreciation for, how forms of inquiry can be understood from a design perspective. It can also be helpful as an analytic tool, when your purpose is to determine the basis of the particular design that underlies a specific approach to inquiry. For example, you are able to examine various design approaches, and reveal the different assumptions that are built into their systems of inquiry and action, utilizing this conceptual lens.

Even though we have primarily focused on the notion that design inquiry and action reside in the domain of the real, design inquiry is, in actuality, an emergent, compound form of inquiry that is inclusive of the real, the true and the ideal as well. All three of these forms of inquiry are essential to designers, and their work. When used together, the resulting approach to knowledge acquisition is much more synergistic, comprehensive and integrative than the individual approaches taken in summation (see Fig. 1-4). Therefore, design inquiry displays emergent qualities as *a consequence of being a compound* that would not be visible and accessible otherwise.

Concomitant with design inquiry is design action. Design action is both a journey and a destination. The journey has to do with change, and the destination with ends, or outcomes. Change is a term with many meanings. One of the most important definitions of change—which has considerable importance in a design context—is that which denotes the process of coming *into* existence, a birthing, genesis or creation. This attribute of change is dramatically different

41

from the more common use of the term, which states that change is a distinguishing difference in the already existing. We should note that change, as a difference *in* something, is also distinctly separate from a difference *between* things, which is essentially the definition of information.

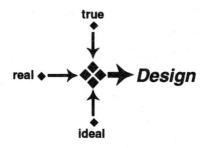

Fig. 1-4 Design Inquiry: An Emergent Compound

Change is initiated differently depending on which form of inquiry is dominant in any situation (see Fig. 1-5). The triggers also vary depending on the type of change; whether it is part of a process of coming into existence, or whether it is transforming that which is in existence already.

As stated earlier, scientific inquiry focuses on change that is triggered by chance and necessity. Statistics and probability theories deal with change caused by chance, while laws, principles and rules define change brought by necessity. Change that is triggered in response to the demanding norm of an idealized standard—the ideal—is often attributed to some form of sovereign or controlling authority that can range from the Word of God to mere peer pressure or expert opinion.

Change that is triggered by human intention is at the heart of design. It is a hallmark of design that human intention is essential and central to instigating the change process.

Designs of Inquiry & Action

	the real	*the true*	*the ideal*
change	human intention	chance & necessity	sovereign intervention

Fig. 1-5 Triggers for Change

Human intention is, therefore, a cause of change. The idea of cause is complex, but key to understanding designed change. Cause is natural (as defined by science, through the conceptualization of chance and necessity). Design, therefore, must accommodate change brought about by natural causes, but the most challenging forms of cause are those that are rooted in human intention. These intentional forms of cause are diverse. The type of intentional cause that is of particular interest here is design cause. Design cause is the consequence of human agency and the capacity for humans to be proactive and purposeful in their interaction with the real world. Design cause is essential both for initiating change that brings new things into existence and for modifying that which is already in existence.

The kinds of outcomes available to a change process vary widely, depending on the inquiry approach being used (see Fig. 1-6). Each form of inquiry has its own ends. The point of intentional change, triggered by design cause, is to bring about a specific, desired end.

43

Designs of Inquiry & Action

	the real	the true	the ideal
	that-which-is-desired-to-be	that-which-can-be	that-which-should-be
ends	that-which-is-not-yet	that-which-is	that-which-ought-to-be

Fig. 1-6 Design Ends

The most obvious outcome of inquiry is knowledge. The type of knowledge, or *knowing*, that is made available as an outcome is determined by the primary mode of inquiry (see Fig. 1-7). For example, a fundamental type of knowing is knowledge associated with judgment, which is different in kind from most forms of knowledge, because it is knowledge that is inseparable from the knower.

The interesting thing about design knowledge is that it emerges from a conscious not-knowing. By this, we mean that design knowledge—while using reason (conscious knowledge), intuition (hardwired, unconscious knowledge) and imagination (subconscious knowledge) as constituent elements—requires an initial state of intentional ignorance. This state is very much like the Taoist 'empty mind' or the Buddhist 'new mind'. It is the quality of mind that is present during play, when it is important to be completely open to what is emergent in the moment, rather than being preoccupied with past experience, or anticipating a future event.

44

- CONSCIOUS KNOWING — REASON
- UNCONSCIOUS KNOWING — INTUITION
- SUBCONSCIOUS KNOWING — IMAGINATION
- CONSCIOUS NOT-KNOWING — DESIGN THINKING

Fig. 1-7 Design Knowing

Design is about evoking, or creating, the real. But, design has to be grounded in what is already real, as well as what is already true. Since the real is overwhelmingly complex and rich, we are unable to grasp the totality of that complexity and richness solely by using the systems created to reveal what is true and factual. The scientific and analytic tools available to us are not designed to handle the real: at least not in any holistic sense, because, from a design perspective, the real is a whole. Any new design is, therefore, something that is both real and whole. As such, that new design is, by definition, too complex and rich to be completely understood during the process of creation. We cannot predict with accuracy how any real design will serve the world and, in turn, how it will change it.

What we can do, is begin to understand that the real—as is manifested in both the particular and the ultimate particular—is a concept that distinguishes design from other traditions of inquiry and action. The real must be approached through judgment (see *Judgment* chapter) augmented by science-based tools and methods. Design thinking, to be accepted as a legitimate decision-making process and foundation for leadership, needs to be grounded in the tradition of science and truth, but not to the exclusion of the tradition of judgment-based reality, or the normative tradition of the ideal. To reiterate, there is a need to combine what is true, ideal and real into a balanced relationship; a compound that incorporates multiple dimensions of the designer's palette.

2. SERVICE

Design is different from other traditions of inquiry and action in that *service* is a defining element. Design is, by definition, a *service relationship*. All design activities are animated through dynamic relationships between those being served—clients, surrogate clients (those who act on behalf of clients), customers and end users—and those in service, including the designers. Design is about *service on behalf of the other*. This is not always obvious when observing the behavior of typical professional designers; neither is it sufficiently dealt with in the contemporary writings on design.

The presence of a binding service relationship in design contributes to a clear distinction between the tradition of design and the traditions of art or science. Science and art are essentially cultures of inquiry and action that are, in the best sense, *self-serving*. Scientists are motivated by their own curiosity and pursue their passion for knowing, in order to satisfy their curiosity objectively. Their gift is a subsequent knowledge that may be of use, somehow, at some point in human affairs. Artists express their passions, feelings and understandings of the world out of their own need for self-expression. Their gift is that these insights are shared with audiences who can then make what they will of these personal glimpses into the human condition. The designer, on the other hand, is not self-serving, but *other-serving*. We should note that it is possible for designers to choose themselves as the client, the one to be served, but that is a special case.

Being in service does not mean being a servant, or subservient. It does not mean acting as a mere facilitator on behalf of someone else's needs. Nor does service exclude self-expression. It just means that self-expression is not dominant in a design relationship, as it is in the traditions of science and art.

We should also point out that service is not about helping people create what they already know they want. The success of the design process can best be determined when those being served experience the *surprise of self-recognition*. This comes when that which emerges from a design process meets and exceeds the client's original expression of that which they (usually only dimly) perceived as desirable in the beginning. This original expression of what is desired is known as the client's *desiderata*. The designer's role is to midwife that desiderata, which could not have been imagined fully from the beginning, by either client or designer and to provide end results in the form of an *expected unexpected* outcome.

Now, what do we mean by this paradoxical expression? We are saying that to contract with a designer has the double intention of both wanting the expected and desired outcome, but also hoping to be surprised with the unexpected. More specifically, an unexpected result that is still recognizable as something that is in resonance with what is desired. The client will, if the design is done in service to that client, understand that the outcome is something new, but at the same time, something fitting the particular situation.

A service relationship is a distinct, complex and systemic relationship, with a particular focus on responsibility, accountability and intention. Designed products, whether concrete or conceptual, only have value and meaning, because of this intentional service relationship. Therefore, it is through the presence of a service relationship that intentional change, and the consequences of intentional change, can come to have meaning and give meaning to individual and

48

collective lives. To a designer, a service relationship is the basic teleo-logical cause of design.

There is a subtle distinction here between designs that are done *with* clients and those that are done *at* clients, like customers or consumers. In the latter case, which is not a service relationship as described above, meaning is discovered through persuasion or through the experience of use. There is also intentional change that is done *to* people. Acts of terrorism or forced changes in their way of life requires that meaning be made in reaction to intention brought against people—the quintessential opposite of service. Unintentional change, such as accidents, natural catastrophes, or the death of a loved one, requires meaning to be made, not because of intention, but in the absence of intention. An example in this last case is that humans have developed grieving processes as a way to secure meaning in the face of irretrievable loss.

It is important, at this juncture, to make a distinction between 'finding meaning' in things that happen, and 'making meaning' by causing things to happen. The former is reactive and adaptive, while the latter is proactive and intentional. To be in service is to be pro-active. This means the designer cannot wait around for things to spontaneously happen, as wished for by the client. Clients may not fully know what is concretely desired in the beginning. They are only aware that something is pressing for expression. This expression of their desiderata may even be masked by feelings of discomfort (for those who lack a critical self-awareness). In this case, the designer must help bring to the surface a clearer articulation of a client's desiderata as a positive, proactive impulse.

This is not always easy to do, as there are often feelings of anxiety concerning the future, and fears of unknown contexts or situations in life. People, in general, prefer what is known or predictable. For instance, a great deal of effort and resources is expended by organizations (public and private) to predict the future (*futuring*) while being fully aware that most major unintended changes in history have come as total surprises (e.g., the fall of the Berlin Wall), taking even experts by surprise. The future is shown repeatedly to be unpredictable. It is only determined by chance and necessity or formed by intention. Intentional futures are brought into existence through the triggering affect of desiderata.

A designer, therefore, 'makes meaning' for a client by empathetically drawing out his or her pre-formed desires. This designer does not ask the client what fully-formed outcome is to be designed, but instead—through open communication—tries to discern the underlying intentions of that client's vaguely-cloaked desiderata—intentions that, most often, are not yet fully recognized by the client. To be in service means to build on these gossamer findings of purpose and to concretely conceptualize them in such a way that they surpass the client's own knowledge and imagination, while fully representing his or her authentic self-interests.

Design outcomes do not have to be virtuous to be considered authentic consequences of design activity; although, one hopes this is, most often, the case. Some individuals may desire only to maximize their material wealth, personal power, or prestige, while others are truly interested in designing a more meaningful life for themselves. One business may endeavor only to increase profit and assure market dominance and longevity. Yet another may desire to contribute something of lasting social value. Some governments may attempt to democratically respond to diverse ways of life, almost as readily as other governments attempt to impose paternalistic control. A good design approach does not assure that 'good' designs emerge as a consequence. Designers—not design approaches—are ultimately responsible for creating altruistic designs.

Our intent, in *The Design Way*, is not to create one-size-fits-all templates, formulas, or prescriptive principles in which to guide design decision making. Rather, we submit that a client's desiderata can best be encountered through an approach that is inclusive of both theoretical and practical knowledge; one that is reflective and experiential, and results in a virtuous design. Through a service relationship, a design is considered successful when the expected-unexpected outcomes serve the right people, for the right purpose, at the right time.

It is important to understand that service is not servitude. Instead, service treats the other as an *equal*. This does not mean being *similar*, as in categories of social science, or *equivalent*, as in egalitarianism, but *equal*, in the sense that anyone's desiderata can become the seed for purposeful change. Service is also distinct from *helping*, which, by its very nature, creates a unilateral relationship. In a helping relationship, all power and resources reside with the 'helper', leaving the 'helpee' in a position of being indebted:

> Serving is different from helping. Helping is based on inequality; it is not a relationship between equals. . . Service is a relationship between equals. . . . Helping incurs debt. When you help someone, they owe you one. But serving, like healing, is mutual. There is no debt.

N. Remen (1996)

In our Western culture, helping relationships are one of the more popular—and self-reinforcing—types of contracts available. Non-

51

profits, governmental agencies and NGOs (non-governmental organizations) spend millions of dollars on behalf of the helpless, sick, unlucky, or tragedy-struck. In many instances, this may be necessary, when there are no good alternatives within easy reach and there seems to be more than sufficient justification for an urgent, unilaterally triaged intervention into the lives of others.

As a consequence, philanthropy and related approaches of 'doing good' have often walked a well-worn path that leads to the formation of habitually unequal relationships. These quick fix, helping relationships tend to prevent service relationships from forming when possible, and where appropriate. Those who have the power and resources to define norms often treat people who are culturally, socially, or economically different as simply needy or helpless. This is also true of individuals who find themselves victims of unhappy circumstances formed by well-intentioned, but misguided, fixes that have resulted in unintended consequences. Although their circumstances are the result of forces outside of their personal sphere of influence, they are treated as the loci for a helping or fixing intervention.

Well-meaning benefactors spend a great deal of their money and influence in these pseudo-contract relationships. As a result, there is a symbiotic relationship between the recipients and the providers. Often the providers, quite unconsciously perhaps, use the helpless and powerless to build a deeper sense of purpose and meaning in their own lives. In other cases, the helpless are there to be taken care of in order that the provider's status—often in reference to power or success—can be legitimized, or justified, in social contexts.

The spenders need a clear and urgent call-to-arms in order to mask the more difficult and challenging job of dealing with the human condition in all of its complexity and potential. This includes dealing with any other human as an equal in diversity. Everyone feels rewarded, at some level, in a helping relationship defined by urgency. Important values, such as caring and love, can form the basis for the best of these relationships. However, this is usually at the expense of other important human values, including those that support dignity, equity, creativity and individuality.

Interestingly, even though service is a defining characteristic of design, some design professions are not framed within this tradition. Architecture, for instance, can be approached from the science, or art, tradition and not forfeit its character as architecture. As we noted earlier, architecture is often referred to as a midpoint between art and science—with these two traditions represented as extreme poles on a continuum. Other fields, such as product design and information systems design, are thought of as a mix of 'hard' science and art. As proponents for a design culture, we would suggest that, rather than classifying these professions as somewhere between the traditions of science and art, they should instead be recognized as professions in the *tradition of design.*

Whether or not architecture, industrial design, information systems design, or any other design profession is to be approached from a design tradition is an entirely intentional choice. However, the consequences of this choice are significant to the praxis of the profession. This can be best exemplified by taking a look at the educational philosophies that have historically supported each of these professions. Education in art is radically different from science education. The values and structure upon which each educational process is built vary significantly. Science pedagogy differs from art pedagogy in that the purpose of education in science is to learn how to determine the true nature of the material world through augmented and controlled input from the natural senses. The outcome is objective and factual knowledge that is confirmed because others can replicate it. On the other hand, art education is about learning to give self-expression to emotions and feelings without the intervention of formal, replicable intellectual constructs. The outcome in this case is subjective and personalized knowledge.

For design to be accepted as its own intellectual tradition, designers must foster their own unique approach to education, as science or art have done so successfully; one that places a priority on the idea of service. The purpose of design pedagogy is, therefore, to learn how to gain both objective and subjective understanding on behalf of another's interests rather than in one's self-interest. It also includes the reintegration of reflective thought and practical action in a way that reintegrates the knowledge of 'why' with the knowledge of 'how'.

If a generative service relationship is one of the higher goals in design, then how a designer communicates with his or her client takes on immense importance. Design communication is about listening. It is about helping people to express what they believe will help them live fuller lives. In order to do this, design communication may at times include the use of rhetoric and persuasion, as is true of science and art. But these forms of argument are not a part of its essential nature. Also, a good designer does not spend time convincing clients of needs or desires they have not authored. So, 'selling', in a traditional marketing sense, is not seminal to the design process. It is the client's own intentionality—in the form of their desiderata—that triggers the process.

When a service relationship is established correctly, it brings everyone involved along at the same pace. Design communication, therefore, does not depend on selling outcomes as much as it does *communicating progress*. Design is, at its root, a form of *democracy*. Not the arithmetic democracy of majority rule or the representative democracy of elected political bodies, but the democracy of self-determination through inter-relationships of service. Design is the kind of democracy that can embrace the growing diversity and complexity of human interests in today's world. Design provides the possibility that each and every person's individual good can be considered, within the framework of the common good.

Therefore, service, in terms of design, demands a heightened and refined ability to 'listen'. To hear what is *pressing for expression* as much as what is being outwardly expressed. To do this, we must utilize *notitia* (Hillman, 1992). Notitia is an act of attention that is complete and uncompromising. One that senses every nuance and can bring into focus details and patterns of connection that elude more passive encounters with real-world situations. Notitia allows a relationship of true empathy to form between the server and served. Notitia is not a method, but a way of being that is highly focused and attentive in the extreme. It is a process of focusing in the way that eyeglasses bring things into clarity (i.e., focus) rather than as a restricting or narrowing of perspective (i.e., focused). It is the opposite of detachment and separation encouraged by contemplative traditions. It is an awareness that is open to all input rather than selective of predefined input as exemplified by expertise (*notitia* is further discussed in the *Splendor of Design* chapter).

Design communication is a complex process that is multi-dimensional and multi-phased. Communication moves from the initial phase of building *trust* (through conversation), to one of finding *common ground* through dialogue (using logic), and developing a shared or common understanding. The process then allows for the creation of an *uncommon understanding* through what we call *diathenic graphologue* (Greek: *dia-theno*: to show through or let a thing be seen through; and *grapho*: image or representation). Uncommon understanding is the outcome of creative thinking that produces breakthrough insights. These insights are in the form of rich, complex images that are difficult, if not impossible, to apprehend from a single perspective. They cannot be represented in the linear format of text. Creative insights break the established common ground and bring the process back to a need for more dialogue, in order to find new common ground.

The purpose of diathenic graphologue is to let the images of insight become manifest. It is a form of discourse carried on through interpretation and communication of these direct images (as well as derivative images). Diathenic graphologue utilizes a broad variety of image formations, including those produced by the imagination itself as well as images concretized in the form of cognitive art. It also enables images created through the intimacy of creative agency to be exchanged with others. This sharing of rich images enables the emergence of a common new understanding, paving the way for a collaborative realization of a newly designed whole. When executed correctly, the three phases listed above—building trust, finding common ground and creating uncommon understanding—constitute a successful design communication process (more on this process is found in the *Imagination and Communication* chapter).

Since the core social tie in the design process is between designers and their clients, a designer needs to be in a balanced and proportioned relationship with the client. Unfortunately, it is not uncommon that this pivotal relationship is distorted. To illustrate this point, we will compare five generalized types of relationships, four unbalanced

56

types and one dynamically balanced type (see Fig. 2-1). Two of these unbalanced relationships, the *designer artist* and the *designer facilitator*, represent very simple relationships where one of the two roles completely dominates the relationship.

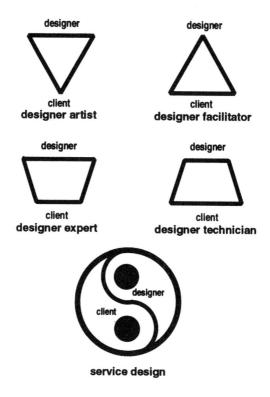

Fig. 2-1 Designer/Client Relationships

In the *designer artist* case, the designer has complete influence over the process and the client has little to none. The designer is not interested in the desires or needs of the client. Instead, he or she creates a design

57

based on his or her own judgments concerning the requirements for a satisfactory design solution. The designer acts in the same way as an artist, where the need to express one's own self is at the core of the relationship. We often see this type of designer being glorified as a 'prima donna', or celebrity designer. Clients who desire prestige, or status, by being identified with high profile designs, often seek out this type of design relationship.

The opposite situation occurs in a *designer facilitator* relationship, where the designer simply 'obeys' any and all requests coming from the client. In this situation, it is accepted that the client knows precisely what he or she wants or needs, and knows specifically what should be done as a consequence—without any input from the designer. The client is, in this case, the sole creative agent in the design process. The designer becomes merely a facilitator. Although facilitation is an important part of any process, it is not the primary role of a designer.

The remaining two forms of unbalanced relationships represent disproportional situations, where either the designer or the client has a majority of influence. In the *designer technician* relationship, we see designers acting simply as technicians; by that we mean they don't contribute intentionally, or creatively, to any part of the design process. Instead, they answer questions, or respond to wishes from an intentional client, acting as an instrumental agent only.

In the *designer expert* relationship, we see the opposite, where the client is called to respond to initiatives taken by the designer. The designer enters the design process as an expert, with predetermined insights and outcomes in hand, dismissing the necessity of customized interactions with the client. As an expert, the designer determines which generalized solution, or solutions, will be adapted to the particular situation of the client.

It is difficult to find an accessible way to visualize the full complexity of a balanced relationship between designers and the clients. To symbolize the ideal *service design* relationship, we have borrowed from the Chinese Yin-Yang model, which shows an intricate relationship where both sides are fully and authentically engaged in a dynamic design process. Both roles—designer and client—are *inclusive of a part of the other*. It is a balanced relation, but it is not a relation without tensions. The model shows that tension is at the core of the relationship. It is in the complexity of the relationship, and in the tension between its different qualities, that imaginative and innovative design work takes place. The model also illustrates that mutual respect is vital to any effective design relationship.

Unlike the majority of group process theories of collective activity, the designer-client service tradition is not an egalitarian relationship, or a hierarchical relationship. These relationships are problem-focused. Instead, design is an inclusive activity, consisting of a *composition of formalized roles* that center on the idea of service. This integrative principle should guide the formation of design teams—creating a complex web of relationships with others who are, in one way or another, a part of the design process. The composition of roles is always unique. In any design situation, this composition has to be considered in the earliest stages of the design process.

It is key to point out that in a service relationship, the designer is responsible to more than just the client, and must assume accountability for others who will be affected by any particular design activity. This includes stakeholders (those who are affected by an intentional change, but who are not included as part of the design process),

stockholders, decision-makers, producers, end users, customers and
surrogate clients (those who, when served, indirectly serve clients
who are unable to represent their own interests). In addition, depending on the nature of what is being created, the designer may even need
to consider future generations and the natural environment.

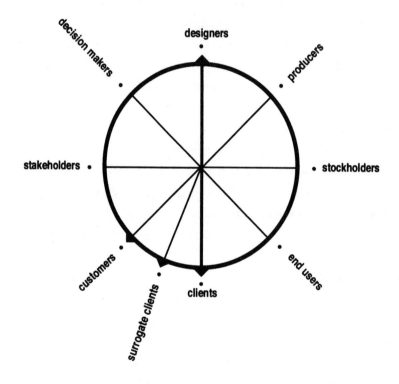

Fig. 2-2 Design Roles

As we examine the service tradition in detail, it becomes quite obvious
that service relationships are far more diverse and comprehensive than

60

the singular relationship that exists between a client and a designer (see Fig. 2-2). The differing relationships among design roles, as presented below, are not exclusive of each other. The relationships among any particular set of roles, in any specific situation, can be compound ones, consisting of several different types. In some cases, it may be appropriate to treat a set of relationships as one-dimensional, but this should always be a matter of intentional choice.

Which of these roles are relevant to a particular design situation should be determined in the contracting process. Identifying which roles will be necessary to satisfy the design goal is the responsibility of the designer(s), in collaboration with those being served. We would suggest that a designer evaluate each relationship carefully, as the essential nature of many roles may not be immediately apparent to everyone involved. We should note, these service relationships are also uniquely defined by the quality of each particular inter-relationship.

The *composition of relationships*, for any given design activity, needs to be intentional. It must be, in effect, designed. The resulting composition(s) can be shown graphically (see Fig. 2-3). Although graphic representations like these fail to show the full complexity and richness of the corresponding relationships, they do make it quite clear that, in every design situation, the possible compositions of relationships are almost infinite.

This being the case—and given the fact that there are no hard-and-fast rules as to what compositions are most beneficial for any particular design situation—each configuration must spring from a designer's intentional design. It is also useful for that designer to experiment with different compositions, trying to imagine how these various combinations might influence the design process, and ultimately, the outcome.

61

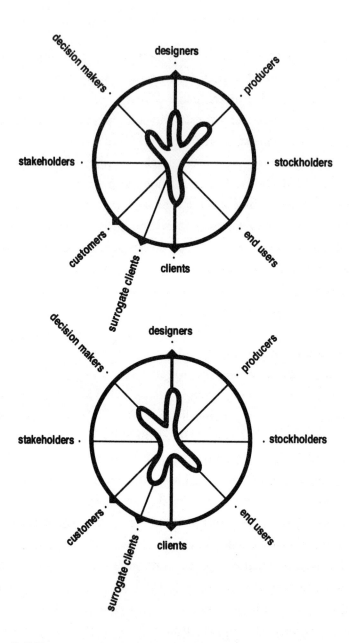

Fig. 2-3 Examples of Intentional Choices of Relationships

Finally, in the process of configuring these relationships, the designer must stay in close communication with the client, remembering that the service relationship between the designer and client is at the core of the process.

As stated earlier, it is not easy to identify all possible roles and relationships. It may not always be that formal or semi-formal roles such as stakeholders, stockholders, decision-makers, producers or makers, end users and customers, are the most suitable roles for a particular design situation. If that is the case, there are other ways of reflecting on relationships. As a designer and/or client, the notion of who 'I' am, in relation to others, could also be thought of as the relation between the conceptual roles of *thou, you, us, them, other, it, all, we, self* (see Fig. 2-4.). There are obviously many other roles of relationship that can be imagined and developed. Choosing which are most appropriate for any particular design situation is a matter of design judgment.

Fig. 2-4 Design Relationships

A relationship, such as *I-you*, is very different in quality from the relationship of *I-other*. Building on some of Erick Jantsch's basic work, as influenced by Martin Buber and others (Jantsch, 1975), the qualities of relationships found in *I-it*, and *I-thou*, can be usefully modified and expanded, giving rise to other forms of relationships such as *I-us*, *we-other* and *all-them*. In addition, other combinations and permutations can be created that would be specifically appropriate for different design situations (Fig. 2-5).

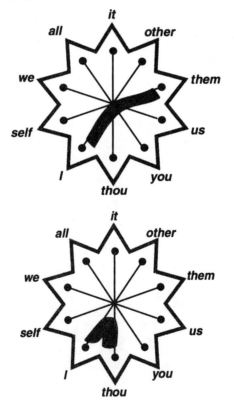

Fig. 2-5 Examples of Design Relationships

For example, as a designer in an *I-us* relationship, the designer becomes a member of the client category and thus is serving in two roles. A designer in an *I-it* relationship treats the client as an objective, impersonal entity revealed primarily through hard data. A designer in an *I-thou* relationship interacts with the client subjectively, with emotion and feeling. A designer in an *I-them* relationship treats the client as an objective but human 'other', fully utilizing insights gleaned from the social sciences. For these and any other set of relational roles, the interaction is different in kind and degree. Each set of relationships forms a social system that must be intentionally designed with the particulars of each design situation in mind. Once again, designers must beware.

The way these relationships are prioritized and rationalized will strongly influence who takes part in the process, and under what conditions. It will affect the role of the designer and what will be expected from all parties. Too often, design processes are disrupted by emergent relationships not planned for ahead of time. A great deal of time and energy must be spent on redefining the composition of the team, requiring that the design process be repeated over again.

Service is a full partnership between those being served and a design team, working in a *conspiracy* (i.e., a breathing together). This configuration forms a tensional, but collaborative, social system. Formal and informal agreements, or contracts, govern such design conspiracies. A design contract is a formalized relationship, where there is an equivalent exchange of value.

Such a contract can be between individuals who actually sit down in real time and negotiate a signed agreement (this is known as *legal contracting*). But, a design contract can also be formed between a designer and others, who are unable to represent themselves personally, such as future generations, those in ill health, or those handicapped in some way by external circumstances. These contracts need to be built on alternative, conceptual principles of agency that are made explicit. For every contract, the designer must determine the moral and legal grounds for assuming agency on behalf of a client who is unable to negotiate directly. Such an agreement is known as *value contracting*.

In any contractual relationship, one needs a clear understanding, based on agreement and consent, of the intention of the contract. There are many types of contract intentions that are often categorically different from one another. For example, below we compare four basic types of contracts, based on intentionality. These intentions include those that are scientific, helpful, art-oriented and service-related (see Fig. 2-6).

The service type of contract is the primary contract in design, although aspects of the other types may be appropriate, in different proportions, depending on the situation. These contracts are often conceptual and do not necessarily represent a legal document. However, they do define a fiduciary relationship where there is an equal exchange of value for agency. These contracts can exist between designers and clients who are unable to represent themselves and their desires in person (such as future generations), but who are represented by surrogates acting indirectly or directly in their stead.

It is important to note that even when there is a desire for intentional change, often one of the non-service contracts are drawn up by default. For instance, if a specific action needs to be taken into consideration for a certain situation, a science approach, which consists of describing, explaining, predicting and controlling, is often employed. This approach, however, is not the kind of approach that supports making design judgments. Science provides descriptions and explanations, but it does not provide a basis for overall judgments, especially in situations where knowledge and information are not complete—which is always the case in design.

Design is limited in time and resources, unlike science, which in theory has an undefined period of time to determine what is true and accurate about a specific area of interest. Scientific research always creates more questions than it answers. Decision-makers who ask that more studies be done before a decision can be reached are confronted with the emergence of more options rather than the desired convergence towards a single best option.

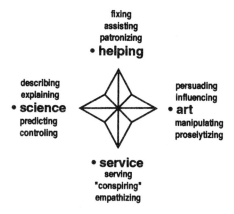

Fig. 2-6 Contract Intentions

The intentionally driven relationships that are built in a service contract, where one is serving, empathizing and 'conspiring', form the binding forces of an effective design team. This team boasts a composition of diverse roles, which are distinctly different, but always

67

equitable, in character. Because of this, those in the role of 'client' experience change motivated out of their own desiderata, rather than someone else's diminished understanding of what is best for them. The client, in this case, is a full member of the design team. There is no assumption of inequity in their capacity to contribute.

This notion of conspiracy transcends mere management of group process. It is similar to the concept of 'flow' in the creative process, as presented by Csikszentmihalyi (1990), where normal divisions and distinctions of everyday activity blend into a seamless experience of intentionality.

This symbiotic relationship is possible only if there is an exchange of empathy. Empathy, in the case of a design situation, is the ability to 'be' as the other, while remaining a whole self. It is the ability to stand in someone else's place while standing on your own. These empathetic states of alignment are then given direction through the emerging understanding of desiderata—an understanding that occurs during the process of serving.

So, to summarize, a designer needs to be able to form intentional service contracts with constituents—i.e., members of a whole. Design contracting is therefore not so much about agreements and exchanges *between* people, as *among* people. He or she must keep in mind how dramatically contracts can vary, and should be sure that his or her client is also clear on the expectations that spring from a particular contract. This way, the two are aligned and integratable going into the process.

In addition, a designer needs to remember the complexity of relationships a service contract entails, and must intentionally engage in a process of designing the team's compositional makeup in response.

68

Lastly, a designer must be willing to let empathy lead the way. This assures that an appropriate design situation will emerge where contracts are formed, relationships built and design goals are guided by focusing on desires and open communication.

3. SYSTEMS

Design can now be taken seriously in domains well outside of the established confines of the craft traditions and the related professional fields that create our material culture. A design approach can be taken in complex, unstructured situations that cut across traditional, disciplinary boundaries because of the development and maturation, over the past few decades, of systems thinking, the *rational component of design.*

In this chapter, systems thinking is presented in two ways. The first introduces the systems approach as the rational activity leading to a systemic outcome or artifact as part of the designing process. The second is the use of a systemic approach to the idea of design itself and the designer's choice of approach. Because of the distinctive methodical tone of this chapter, it has a different feel than the other chapters; nevertheless, it fits into an essential overall understanding of design. Its contribution to design understanding may be easier to grasp after first reading the remaining chapters and then returning to this one.

The design approach has two major cognitive components in its overall designing strategy. One is a compound of imaginative, intuitive, emotional and instinctive thinking, manifested as design judgments. The second is a compound of reasoning, inclusive of both analytic and synthetic thinking. Synthetic thinking has become particularly effective in the new design tradition because of the availability of more fully developed systems scholarship. Analytic thinking is equally effective in design reasoning, but there is a caution.

The challenge in design is to not allow analysis to become the dominant or exclusive rational thinking process.

The benefits of analytic (i.e., scientific) thinking are often accompanied by the disastrous effects of logical dissection as a means of studying the elements, components or qualities of things in isolation from their intact whole. Emergent qualities displayed as patterns, compounds, functional assemblies, wholes or compositions disappear when disassembled into constituent parts. Wetness, a quality associated with water, is an emergent quality resulting from the combination of atoms of hydrogen and oxygen. Wetness disappears as an attribute when a water molecule is reduced to its constituent atoms. Life, as an emergent quality of biologic systems, disappears when the living plant or animal is dissected into elemental components. Abstract entities, such as community or family, similarly lose their emergent qualities when divided into individuals for analysis. The point of a work of art disappears altogether when categories of materials and methods are studied individually through decomposition.

The benefits that the scientific tradition has bequeathed to Western Civilization are tremendous, but they come with some fairly risky strings attached. Scientific, or analytic, approaches to understanding the world—through a consistent dedication to reductive observation and analysis—have provided powerful insights, helpful in predicting and controlling nature, for the betterment of humanity. But these gifts also have negative consequences, both to nature and to humans, as mentioned above.

Nature is not merely a collection of organic and inorganic elements or compounds, possessing attendant qualities and attributes, which exist in isolation. Nor is humanity merely a collection of individuals in isolated proximity to one another. Everything is in relationship to everything else with varying levels of criticality and intensity. These relationships produce qualities and attributes at multiple levels of resolution. Complexity, a distinctive attribute arising as a consequence of the dynamic interactivity of relationships, is the rule in the real world, while simplification or reductionist thinking, such as ignoring relationships and concomitant emergent qualities, is a dangerous distraction. Analytic, reductionist thinking (separating into parts for the purpose of study) can create knowledge that is powerful and productive in a positive way only when brought back into a context of inquiry that takes into account the existence of complex relationships and the phenomenon of emergence (to make analog).

Elemental states, perceived as independent from an analytic perspective, are actually quite interdependent in significant ways; ways which generally guarantee their own continued existence. Everything exists in an environment and within a context. Everything depends on other things for something, whether it is food, protection, or other basic needs. Such assemblies of functional relationships lead to the emergence of phenomena that transcend the attributes and qualities of the things themselves. Ecosystems are one example of this. An ecosystem, as a community of living things in close interaction with one another, displays qualities that are experienced only in aggregation, as in the case of wet lands. This type of ecosystem filters and purifies the water that flows through it as a result of the complex interaction of the plants and animals that inhabit it. Another example of emergence is a house, a functional assembly of construction materials, until it is experienced holistically as a home—not merely a building. Since life itself is an emergent quality, an attribute of functional organic assemblies, it is literally life threatening, when dealing with living systems, for relationships to be ignored or broken through the intervention of reductive thinking or action.

Another critical shortfall of the reductionist approach concerns the separation of function from purpose in conceptual analysis. Reductionist approaches in thinking and intervention separate and isolate function from teleological ends. But what we argue here is that the understanding and improvement or optimization of functional members of a system in isolation from the purpose or ends of a system is not possible. The relationships between functional activity and teleological considerations are as important as the relationships between system elements. An approach that assures that critical consideration of relationships and emergence are accounted for is necessary to overcome this and other limitations of reductionist thinking.

When we view nature and human activity as interrelated and inter-relating, we are taking a *systems approach*, which is opposite to the reductionist approach described above. As designers, we believe that we need to view the world from this systems perspective. *The systems approach is the logic of design.* Such an approach requires that close attention be paid to relationships and the phenomenon of emergence when evaluating any subset of existence. If the designer's intention is to create something new, not to just describe and explain, or predict and control, it is especially important to take a systems approach.

There is no way around the fact that any design created will be in relationship to, and interrelated with, the real world. From a systems perspective, all successful designs are compositions of elemental parts in interrelated relationships that evoke the emergence of desired qualities in the design itself, while attending to the sustainability of the design, through adaptive purpose, in its ever-changing

74

environment. A physical example of such a design is the DC-3 airplane. This plane, as the first of its kind, was not only functionally exceptional at the time it was first introduced in 1933, but it has continued to successfully serve the needs of owners and users well beyond its expected life span as an industrial artifact. It is continuing in service to this day, despite overwhelming changes in the aircraft industry and aviation field.

Another way of illustrating the importance of a systems approach in design is to contrast that which is essentially analog in character, with that which is digital or analytic. As defined earlier, by analog we mean a form, process or experience that is perceived as undifferentiated and continuous, as opposed to the discontinuity imposed by a digital or analytic perspective. For example, the human condition, both in a natural and historical context, is analog when life is experienced as a flow. 'Meaning making' in human experience is dependent on being contained within this analog context. Things make sense only when connected and interrelated. If things occur without connection in a discontinuous way, there is no inherent meaning present. Meaning is only attributed to that which is put into relationships in context. This is what a systems perspective does for design. Design is a process of meaning making because it is engaged in creation from a systems perspective, holistically and compositionally.

It is only in the most recent, infinitesimal fraction of the human lifeline, when technologic cultures have pushed to the fore, that the analog experience of life has not been dominant. In some great cultures like that of China, the analog was able to remain dominant, even during the great analytic or digital transformation of the last century, though in recent years, it has slowly embraced a more digital perspective. How can a society not change, when the success of the analytic and digital in the material development of the West is so undeniable? But, we would argue that the negative consequences of not reintegrating these scientific approaches back into an analog life experience are becoming more and more apparent. Hydroelectric dams that interrupt the migration routes of salmon are one example. Both fish and humans have to go to great lengths to get around (both figuratively and literally) the disruptive effects of these dams. Examples such as this show how an analytic and digital perspective of reality typically only depicts some aspect of the complexity and richness of the analog world.

Much of modern life is experienced as a fractured and stressful whirlwind. The lack of integration between analytic design systems and our own analog life experience can be seen as the primary reason for the current levels of angst and yearning in individuals—a longing for a more integrated, meaningful and holistic life experience. The challenge for designers is to take advantage of the benefits of the analytic in their design approaches, while at the same time integrating these elements into an overall compositional approach, which draws from the analog.

These new designs are then introduced into the world as analog contributions to the human experience, rather than as simply attached, meaningless elements. Design can be served by the analytic and digital, but it must finish out as an analog composition, in order to fit back into the human experience. One excellent example of this is the way in which the traditional Balinese culture integrates artistic representation, agricultural processes and spiritual ritual into an undifferentiated, holistic, lived experience. For example, a newly designed rice plant introduced into the agricultural sector would be quickly integrated into the totality of the analog Balinese life experience, because the Balinese do not partition their lives into distinct categories such as religion, work, art and community. They maintain seamless lives in contrast to Westernized cultures.

Let us restate the point that design as a human activity has many distinct challenges. One of the most important is the ability to move from an integrated analog reality—through a phase of analytic understanding digitally expressed—and then back to an analog experience, which then coherently integrates a new and purposeful design into the human experience (see Fig. 3-1).

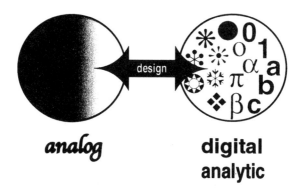

analog   **digital analytic**

Fig. 3-1 Analog to Digital/Analytic Back to Analog

The end products, or artifacts, of design will invariably be *social systems* or *subsystems of social systems*. This is true whatever the actual outcome of the design process (e.g., a product, building, service, process, or abstract concept). This is because all things are related systemically and nothing exists in isolation. Whether an idea or a coffeemaker, it will be fully embedded in a complex system of relationships. Not only are the artifacts systems-related, but the agents of change—the designers and the design teams—are social systems as well. Design roles and relationships are systemic. Design processes are both systemic (integrative and interconnected), and systematic (methodical). This is why it is essential for designers to theoretically understand the nature of systems and for them to use systems thinking as the basis for design reason.

There is another reason for using a systems approach, given that we understand that life is an analog experience. As we've said before, breaking our experience into units of information has been a successful strategy for the introduction of evolution-altering changes into social and cultural realms. However, it has proven to be quite difficult to integrate digitized artifacts back into the natural analog form of experienced life. This means that a digital frame of reference allows human intention and will to enter into a process that is designed to be *experienced and adapted to*, rather than *engaged in purposefully*. A systems approach, and its associated competencies in systems thinking and action, provides the ability to successfully move from the analog to the digital, and back again.

Despite a recent coining of the phrase 'the digital age' to mean our current, and immediate past history, the Western world has actually been digital for the last 750 years (Crosby, 1997). Time, space and energy have all been divided into packets, or abstract forms of information, which prove to be very stable over time. These packets provide information only when they are in a correct relationship with each other. Regardless of the amount of information these packets can provide, it is important to realize *the relationships themselves provide meaning*. Thus, the division of the day into hours, minutes and seconds meters the passage of time without saying what kind of a day it was. A mapping grid demarcates traffic patterns and real estate, but does not

78

delineate the human qualities of neighborhoods, communities, or hometowns. Electrical impulses may be digitized forms of energy, which can convert into digital modes of communication, but they cannot translate the message they are sending.

That is not to say that the ability to digitize the human experience is not a valuable asset to design. In fact, it can be quite helpful in forming and sharing design communications; just as rational analysis (meaning the ability to analyze and understand complex assemblies by separating them into logical sub-assemblies and constituent parts) has proven essential to design analysis. Scientific thinking provides a significant portion of the designer's foundational platform, upon which the entire design process stands.

However, a comprehensive design process ultimately entails the additional process of *composition* (creation of the analog) in order for the resulting design to weave seamlessly back into the human experience. This compositional process, which requires intention and judgment, will ultimately yield an understanding of what we want the analog whole to be like. But, in order to reach this vision, we need an understanding of the analog experience of reality. And, for this, we need *systems thinking*.

The term *system* has many definitions promulgated by a pantheon of contemporary systems thinkers. Sometimes, a systems thinking approach refers to a way of thinking and learning about the human condition (i.e., epistemology). It can also refer to a description and explanation of things that affect the human condition. The latter of these two definitions includes those that promote a scientific approach to understanding systems as 'real things' (i.e., ontology), either concrete or abstract. The former, a systems inquiry approach, focuses on a way of thinking which allows different fields of interest to be related to each other in the affairs of human beings.

Systems thinking is both a very new and very ancient approach to meaning making. Meaning making is essentially the creation of relationships of understanding, specifically between that which is experienced and the one who experiences. These relationships form a belief system, inclusive of the real, the true and the ideal, that informs actions, reflection and imagination in specific situations.

Modern systems approaches are often catalogued as branches of science, such as the study of complex phenomena, or the attempt to unify all rational knowledge. Some contemporary systems thinkers restrict systems ideas to the domain of the newer sciences, such as chaos theory and complexity theory, exclusively. However, C. West Churchman, a well-known systems philosopher, posits that systems thinking has been in use as far back as the *I Ching*. He argues that this ancient Chinese text is, in fact, humanity's oldest systems book (Churchman, 1979). He further points out that historical cosmologies and religions are, in effect, systems approaches to meaning making—approaches that have been life enhancing for generations of human beings. From this perspective, systems thinking can be seen as a very old and fundamental tradition—a tradition that gives form and meaning to the human condition, and which has, unfortunately, given too much way to the powerful attraction of reductionist, analytic thinking.

Recently, systems thinking has frequently been identified with the innovative, but nonscientific, ideas associated with the *New Age* movement. Although it is easy to dismiss many of the 'crackpot' off-shoots of this movement, some of the underlying principles are quite sound and definitely systems related. For instance, the importance of synthesis and integration—as a means of gaining a more comprehensive understanding of reality—is one of the primary motivating principles behind all systems approaches, including those practiced by *New Agers*. One of the more valuable insights this principle brings to systems thinking is an appreciation for the fact that many traditional cultures were and are systemic in nature, even though the language they use to describe their own realities is quite different from the formal systems language developed in the Western tradition.

True to form, the scientific approach treats the scholarly domain of systems theory as a disciplinary field bounded by all the principles and traditions of any disciplined inquiry. This has built-in limitations, as there are key differences between the way most scientific disciplines categorize knowledge and the way knowledge is understood from a systems perspective. The scientific approach to systems research requires the field to use the same formalized procedures as are inherent in all scientific research despite the need to be systemic.

Within the scientific tradition, disciplinary inquiry is based on determining clearly defined relationships of similarity, which, once noted and developed into a body of knowledge, are subsequently, distilled into categories of commonality. Over time, these disciplines have evolved into ever-narrowing specialization that tradition holds will bring increased expertise, and thus, value. These areas of expert knowledge share little common ground. In addition, new disciplines continue to emerge, adding to the number of distinct and separate domains of knowledge.

Any attempt to gain knowledge from a broader, more inclusive perspective is perceived, by disciplinarians, as shallow and dilettantish. This creates a situation where rigor and relevance become difficult to reconcile. Compromise between these two conditions results in fields

81

of knowledge defined as being interdisciplinary or multidisciplinary. For those intrepid explorers mining these new lands, the use of inter-disciplinary knowledge can be extremely daunting within a scientific context, where reverence for 'experts' and expert knowledge is all. How does one satisfy the scientific tradition's demand for increasing specialization in a field such as systems thinking, where the integrative process—by definition—is intended to break down those very same barriers of expertise?

It becomes quite clear that systems thinking is a distinctive form of inquiry that does not fit naturally into the traditional specifications reserved for scientific disciplines. What a systems approach does, instead, is offer an alternative to the forced compromise between narrow specialization, and broad, but shallow, generalization. Systems thinking focuses on relationships between domains of knowledge, and on the patterns of relationship that emerge as a consequence. These patterns provide a map for the development of hybrid forms of knowledge, and for their application in theoretically, and pragmati-cally, relevant ways. These patterns are given meaning through interpretation. This is similar to the scientific tradition, where raw data are also interpreted and then given meaning.

The domain of systems and systems thinking does not have a predefined field of interest, or content area. Like science, art and other traditions of inquiry, it is a lens through which observation, imagination, comprehension, understanding and action are focused on a particular domain of human existence. In this sense, it parallels the design tradition. Some characteristics of systems thinking are essential to and supportive of design (see Fig. 3-2). Taken together, the list is inclusive of ways in which systems thinking can help facilitate the establishment of meaning in design.

Emergence is the coming into being, or appearance, of systems attributes that only exist because of systemic circumstances. It is a form of systemic genesis, whether emerging as a consequence of an accretion of things (*tectonic*) or as a consequence of things being intentionally brought together for a purpose (*architectonic*). Emergence is made manifest through unifying concepts, such as compounds, patterns, wholes and compositions. Emergence provides character or identity to a systemic aggregation. An emergent quality often reveals underlying qualities as well.

EMERGENCE

RELATIONSHIP

ORGANIZATION

CONSILIENCE

SUBSTANCE

FORM

PURPOSE

COMPLEXITY

DISTINCTION

CONTRIVANCE

COMMUNICATION

Fig. 3-2 Discerning Characteristics of Systems Thinking

Relationship is inclusive of the systemic attributes of connection, affiliation, influence and alliance. These attributes of relationship are further defined by whether they are in a hierarchical form, in a relationship of equality or equivalency, are nested or integrated. Functional relationships and relationships of control are of particular importance in design. Communication and control (i.e., cybernetic) relationships include both positive (amplifying) and negative (suppressing) feedback into the dynamic behavior of a system. From the perspective of design, the most important form of control relationship is *feed-forward* or purpose focused behavior control. Most importantly, relationships are meaningful in that relationships create meaning. Something may have value in and off itself, but unless it is in some kind of inter-relationship with something else, it carries no meaning.

Organization, or that which causes things to stand together as a system, refers to the forces that attract, bind or contain the elements that come to make up a system. There are many ways in which systems are organized. Systems can be organized by being 'assembled' into a system with mechanical or physical connections put into place. Conceptual systems can be organized by the binding effect of an abstract ordering system that creates the intellectual force field of logical connections. There are even theories in which systems emerge through spontaneous self-organization. The necessity and desirability of survival or self-interest may organize social systems as well. Social systems can become organized through the contractual authority of ownership over the system elements and resources. A social system may also be organized in response to the desire to pursue some strategic purpose. From a design perspective, one of the most critical organizing forces is service. Social systems are organized and held together for the purpose of serving the needs and desires of people. Organization in design is basic to design composition.

Consilience—the unity of knowledge—focuses on that which is common or shared across scientific disciplines, the humanities, professions and other traditions of inquiry. It includes those principles, or laws, that are similar in any systemic situation, or that form part of a general theory of systems. It also includes consideration of archetypes of systemic structure, or behavior, that cuts across types of systems in different fields of interest.

Substance relates to the 'prima materia' of physical being, including matter, mass and corporeity, in relation to concrete systems. For abstract systems, it deals with the basic, essential, axiomatic material from which conceptual or theoretical systemic components and assemblies are formed.

Form, a dominant concern for design, is the synthesis of structures, behaviors, boundaries, shapes, spaces and dynamics of systems as real things or of systems approaches as strategies of inquiry. Although form is a synthesis of these different things, each classification is important to design individually. For instance, in the case of systemic boundaries, an important attribute from the design perspective is that of integrity—whether the system is 'open' to exchanging energy and material with its environment and other systems or it is 'closed'.

Purpose, the teleological dimension of systemic behavior, is of particular importance because it is inclusive of design related issues of intention, such as process, function, means and ends. Purpose is used to define classes of systems, as well as ways of intervening in systems. Purpose is integrally linked to design in its formulation as both a process and as a product or outcome.

Complexity, or complexification, concerns the process of inclusion, encompassment, incorporation, assimilation and completeness. It is especially important to note that it is not the same thing as being comprehensive. It is about taking into consideration everything and anything that is judged to be potentially significant. It is a matter of "mixing apples and oranges" and "speaking of cabbages and kings" through the process of pulling everything into relationship and placing them in a shared context. This is done consistently and intentionally, assuring any design situation will be appropriately complex.

Distinction, based on a systemic perspective, is essential in design. It is the means by which the elements or components for a design composition are made clear (made part of the design palette). Important systemic distinctions for design also include the identification of key items such as variables, roles, environmental factors and other particulars.

Contrivance is a particularly important concept in relationship to systems design. Systemic phenomena are not things that exist as coherent wholes prior to being designated as such. They become distinct entities through human designation. They are discretionary constructs made for such reasons as convenience, utility, expedience, aesthetics, fairness and reasonableness. There are many reasons for why or how something is conceptualized as a system. From a design perspective, these decisions or choices are always judgments.

Communication is essential for understanding systems from two different perspectives. The first concerns communication as a dimension of systems cybernetics—a constitutive element in system behavior. Secondly, systems have to be described, explained and represented, in order to be worked with conceptually and presented accurately. In addition, a designer must create a representation of the characteristic and vital qualities of the existing context within which a new design will reside. Systems modeling is invaluable in this process. Although systems approaches differ, a common consideration is that principles, such as relationship, unity and integration, are essential descriptors of any system being studied, or created. *The primary*

86

descriptors utilized by systems thinking delineate emergent qualities, such as pattern, compound, system and composition.

As explained earlier, this belief is in contrast to the scientific method, where the analytic separation of phenomena into constituent parts is the accepted means of approaching knowledge creation. In our culture, it is a continuous challenge to keep the basic intention of systems thinking (e.g., maintaining a focus on emergent qualities, relationship, etc.), without slowly starting to use our systemic tools to work in a reductionist way. Our culture tells us that the more precisely we know the details, the deeper the knowledge we have about specific properties, the better off we are. Therefore, engaging in a real systems thinking mode—with its emphasis on gaining a better understanding of patterns, compounds and compositions—can be a difficult, almost unnatural, task for a designer, but one of supreme importance to the outcome of his or her work.

Representing systems so that the essence of the system, as imagined or observed, can be communicated to others, is a complex and demanding skill. Models, diagrams and other forms of cognitive art are invaluable and essential (Tufte, 1990). Our dominant mode of communication, the linear format of text, falls short when used without the corroboration of other means of representing complex, dynamic entities. Describing, explaining and imagining systems necessitates the ability to represent them, using form, structure and process representations (see *Imagination and Communication* chapter).

For example, systems, including designs of systems of inquiry, can be represented utilizing the concept of *systemic compounds*. A compound is a complex set of interrelated elements, which are combined in unique blends. Coherent and consonant attributes of any particular systemic compound can be revealed indirectly through the means of

87

abstract conceptual images in the form of *reflections*, or *projections*, of particular aspects of the compound. These reflections, or projections, created from a single perspective, are less complex and thus more comprehensible than the whole.

The constituent elements of systemic compounds, when revealed by their isolation as separate parts, is a less satisfactory method for representing systems than that described above, as the familiar fable of the blind men describing an elephant makes clear. In this story, blind men are asked to describe an elephant, which they do by touching it at different places. The one who touches the tusk describes the elephant as a spear, the one who touches the trunk describes the elephant as a snake, the one who touches the elephant's ear describes it as a fan, while the one who grabs the tail describes the elephant as a rope. Obviously, from a sighted person's perspective, none of the descriptions are accurate, nor would a summation of their descriptions render a factual representation of 'elephantness'. Additionally, systemic compounds are revealed partially or vaguely through images, which are distorted by intervening factors or elements that filter or dim direct cognitive access. Filters like culture, habit and expert expectation are unavoidable, requiring allowances to be made.

All systemic compounds exhibit their own unique emergent qualities and behaviors. Systemic compounds represent the substance, but not the *form*, of a design, in the same way that water is the substance of a hydrogen-oxygen compound, while waves or snowflakes are forms. *Patterns, systems and compositions differ from compounds in that they represent form and not substance.*

Systems thinking and the systems approach can be characterized as arising from a mix of different traditional approaches to inquiry and learning, which are combined in certain proportions within the constraints of the given contexts. The emergent systems thinking compound that constitutes design inquiry and action becomes a *world-approach*, in distinction to the way that scientific inquiry for description and explanation forms *worldviews*. An *approach* is action oriented, while *view* is passive and noninterventionist. A world-approach, like design, depends on the reliability of effective worldviews but is inclined towards taking action as well. Design, as a world-approach, emerges as a compound of design *contexts* and *intentions*. For example, in social systems design, the *contexts* would consist of different types of systems perspectives: social, economic, political, religious and legal systems. An example of epistemological (i.e., how one engages in inquiry and learning) *intentions*, in the case of design, is illustrated by the *real, true* and *ideal* as introduced in *The Real* chapter (see Fig. 3-3).

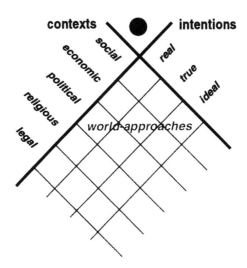

Fig. 3-3 Illustrative Palette of Elements for the Development of Compound World-Approaches

The potential emergent design compounds, or world-approaches, that can be formed from among these contexts and intentions are numerous, with the choice of a particular one being a matter of design judgment. For example, a religious based world-approach can be a compound of both ideal and real intentionality, thus mixing spiritual and practical concerns in a manner that fits more easily into the contemporary life styles found in the technically developed West. Another example would be a political world-approach that is a compound of both ideal and true intentionality, resulting in a science based utopian approach to policy design. Legal world-approaches can be contrasting compounds of true and real intentionality (legal systems based on precedents) and compounds of true and ideal intentionality (legal systems based on codes).

Although complex, systemic world-approaches and worldviews are difficult to formally model or map, they can be imagined as an emergent form which has come into being as a consequence of complex interactions and relationships illuminated against backdrops of multiple, reflective frames of understanding, and meaning making. For example, the concept of *paradigm* creates coherent frames of reference by defining the epistemological rules of the game for any particular system of inquiry. In contrast, world-approaches (and worldviews) can be made visible through the presentation of multiple images that have been projected or illuminated from different station points, by a coherent perspective.

One example of this would be Plato's shadows of idealized forms on a cave wall, where prisoners could only see the shadows of the true forms. Plato's shadows are an example of a single perspective, projecting onto a single cognitive surface. Such a worldview is the most restrictive because it offers only one perspective.

Let's look at another example. When light is studied from two different frames of reference, it becomes clear that the ultimate nature of light is both wave and particle, depending on which image you choose to study. A great deal can be learned about the nature of light from looking carefully at these two images, yet the true composite nature of light remains a mystery.

The Christian trilogy—the Father, Son and Holy Spirit—is an example of three images of one God seen in three different frames of reference, thereby revealing a more in-depth understanding of an infinitely complex deity.

The reflected, or projected, images are always formed by the internal protocols for each frame-of-reference in the same way that individual paradigms dictate the theories that are congruent within its terms. Being able *to create distinct complex images and then conceptually model them in relationship to each other, as a whole, is the function—and ultimately the value—of systems thinking in the design tradition.*

Let's focus on a real-world example of these principles. For example, look at lending policies for new homes. A decision based on these policies may be considered "just good business practice" in an economic frame of reference. At the same time, it may be considered to be unfair in a social frame of reference, or may be treated with total indifference by a legal or political framework, because it was not against the law, nor was it required by law. As you can see, a real-world event, projected onto three different frames of reference, can reveal dramatically different understandings, values and meaning. Yet, at the same time, the incident remains a coherent singular event in the world. One specific event may be seen as a vice from a social point of view, a virtue in the business world and at the same time be treated with complete indifference in the political arena (see Fig. 3-4).

Complex ideas and beliefs are often perceived as paradoxes, when images from two different frames of reference of the same complex thing are viewed together (see Schön & Rein, 1994, for a similar conceptualization). When light is observed as both wave and particle, there is a desire to resolve the paradox into one or the other reality. In the social realm, paradoxes that cannot be resolved by the dominance of one image over the other are resolved by strategies such as compromise, or trade-off. However, attempts to resolve irresolvable differences between images are not the answer, because the images are not based on commensurable perspectives.

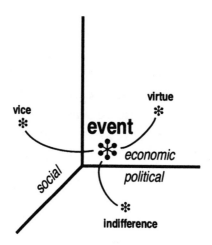

Fig. 3-4 Multiple Images of the Same Event

Instead, the tensions created by an awareness of two or more paradoxical images need to be mediated through a systems approach. We can find an example of just such mediation in Aristotle's concept of the *mean*, the mean being a *mediated* judgment, where understanding emerges from a reconciliation of differences between things, as in the case of a judgment that mediates between mercy and justice.

Unfortunately, without this level of understanding, the tensions and paradoxes of multiple images are too often dismissed out-of-hand. Within reductionistic thinking, the concept of *duality* evokes such a reaction. According to this approach, the *right* way to think is to stay within one frame of reference and act as if the image is a true, undifferentiated form. This is the accepted approach, even when the truth of the image is more complexly comprehensive. Another reductionist alternative is to deal only with pure systems, designed solely from within one frame of reference, and from one perspective. Scientific systems theories which reject the need for concepts such as frame-of-reference and perspective in their inventory of acceptable systems concepts, also reject the possibility of multiple, paradoxical images generated from a singular form. This is the case with *systems science*, which endorses a distilled worldview, as opposed to *systems thinking*, which embraces a more compound worldview.

Systems thinking is both a worldview and a world-approach, depending on whether your intention is to describe and explain, or to act. Systems thinking represents the way people naturally think about the world, accepting without question its wide variations. Reducing images and events into purer—and thus simpler—distillations as prescribed by the scientific method is not only difficult to do, but also hard to maintain, as it is more natural for people to bring their *whole* selves into the daily process of making sense out of life. The whole person is not a distillation. This is important for the designer to remember. Distillations are inherently unnatural—whereas, compound world-approaches and worldviews function in an inherently natural way.

Now, let us look more closely at the term *system*. It has been used as a description of both an 'embodied way of thinking', and of the thing that is being thought *about*. As with the term design, it is both action and an object. The Greek origin of the noun 'system' is *sustema*, meaning a composite whole. When 'system' is used as a modifier of action, its derivative is of the compound term *sunistanai*, which means, 'to bring together' (*sun*—'together' + *histanai*—'to cause to stand'). Thus, a systems thinking approach denotes the desire to know how things are caused to stand together in unity. Therefore, systems design thinking reflects a desire to understand how systems are caused to become compositions and to act on that knowledge as an intentional agent for change.

The term system, as a noun, has been redefined in a number of ways in recent literature. Listed below are a few examples from well-known, contemporary systems thinkers.

> We postulate that systems are examples of teleological things, i.e., things some of whose properties are functional. ...briefly, the necessary conditions that something S be conceived as a system are as follows:
>
> 1. S is teleological.
>
> 2. S has a measure of performance.
>
> 3. There exists a client whose interests (values) are served by S in such a manner that the higher the measure of performance, the

better the interests are served, and more generally, the client is the standard of the measure of performance.

4. S has teleological components which coproduce the measure of performances of S.

5. S has an environment (defined either teleologically or ateleologically), which also coproduces the measure of performance of S.

6. There exists a decision maker who—via his resources—can produce changes in the measures of performance of S's components and hence changes in the measure of performance of S.

7. There exists a designer, who conceptualizes the nature of S in such a manner that the designer's concepts potentially produce actions in the decision maker, and hence changes in the measures of performance of S's components, and hence changes in the measure of performance of S.

8. The designer's intention is to change S so as to maximize S's value to the client.

9. S is "stable" with respect to the designer, in the sense that there is a built-in guarantee that the designer's intention is ultimately realizable.

C. West Churchman (1971)

2.14. System: a set of interrelated elements, each of which is related directly or indirectly to every other element, and no subset of which is unrelated to any other subset.

Hence, a system is an entity composed of at least two elements and a relation that holds between each of its elements and at least one other element in the set. The elements form a completely connected set that is not decomposable into unrelated subsets. Therefore, although a system may itself be part of a larger system, it cannot be decomposed into independent subsystems.

2.15. Abstract system: a system all of whose elements are concepts.

2.16. Concrete system: a system at least two of whose elements are objects.

Russell L. Ackoff and Fred E. Emery (1972)

The systems paradigm is concerned with wholes and their properties. It is holistic, but not in the usual (vulgar) sense of taking in the whole; systems concepts are concerned with wholes and their hierarchical arrangement rather than the whole.

Peter Checkland (1981)

As seen above, a system is defined through a confluence of concepts. According to these authors, a system is located both within a context and an environment, and has a different relationship with each. A system is described as being embedded in a metasystem (i.e., nested within a larger system). A system is also defined as being in relationship to other systems, some of which may compete, cooperate, or influence the system of interest. A system can be profiled in reference to its boundary; whether that boundary is open or closed to things like energy, resources and information, either emerging from within or coming from outside the system. A system is further explained through the identification of its elements, units, subsystems, or other constituent parts. Another descriptor is of the processes that may animate the system. Most importantly, a system is explained through the patterns and qualities of the relationships of its components. A system is further characterized by the emergent properties and behaviors which these patterns and combinations evoke.

The literature is full of descriptions and explanations of immense numbers of systems, all drawn from the perspectives of a wide variety of individual systems practitioners and researchers. There is extensive philosophic, and to a lesser degree, metaphysical literature on systems. Specific systemic processes have been the focus of intense interest, including those involved in communication and control (cybernetics), theories of self-making (autopoiesis) and adaptive or evolutionary behavior. Chaos theory, fractal geometry and complexity theory are all contemporary systems concepts that serve as mathematically sophisticated means for explaining and describing systems. These and other systems-related concepts have been developed in great depth in recent years. Unfortunately, when evaluating these concepts, it is often unclear what basic beliefs about systems theory have been put into play, either from an ontological perspective (the study of the real existence of things), or from a epistemological viewpoint (the study of how knowledge is gained).

Systems are identified in many ways. Even if there is limited utility in knowing all of the different definitions and characterizations of systems, it is important for designers to have a clear understanding of how *they* would define systems, and systems thinking. No designer can practice design and avoid dealing with systems through his or her own understanding of a systems approach.

- SCALE
- HIERARCHY
- FUNCTION
- PURPOSE/ENDS
- MATERIAL
- RATIONAL/LOGICAL DIVISIONS
- THEORETICAL FRAMEWORKS
- KINDS OF COMPONENTS
- TYPES OF VARIABLES
- DEGREES OF COMPLEXITY
- BEHAVIORAL DYNAMICS
- ORDERING LOGIC
- RELATIONSHIPS OF ELEMENTS
- LIMITS

Fig. 3-5 Illustration of Focal Areas for System Categorization

Systems theorists often discern various types of systems by using *descriptive dimensions*. Some of the dimensions, by which systems are recognized or conceptualized, are listed in Figure 3-5. For example, Russell Ackoff categorizes systems as either mechanical, organic, or social (Ackoff & Emery, 1972). Ludwig von Bertalanffy (1968), building on the work of Kenneth E. Boulding, categorizes systems as static structures, clockworks, control mechanisms, open systems, lower organisms, animals, man (sic), socio-cultural systems and symbolic systems.

There are additional categories of systems that have been developed by other systems scholars that provide important insight into the nature of systems and systems approaches (as well as the nature of the inquirers themselves).

Using categories, such as those listed above, systems practitioners have identified untold numbers of systems types. If, by happenstance, you were to be introduced to the field of systems thinking by just *one* of these predetermined systems concepts, it could easily lead to a restricted perspective on the field. A designer is always wise to consider the *a priori* selection of dimensions used in the composition of a systems concept. Although there is some comfort in not being confronted, at the beginning of one's studies, with all the complexities and subtleties of systems thinking as a whole, it is essential for systems designers to appreciate the fullest possible palette of dimensions. The specific types or categories of systems in ordinary usage vary according to specific domains of interest. The list below is an example of the variety of classifications of systems that can be found in widespread usage among systems scholars (see Fig. 3-6). This is by no means an exclusive list, but it does represent some of the many common ways used for sorting and classifying systems. A specific characterization of a system can include aspects of any, or many, of these descriptive dimensions.

Of course, the challenge for a designer is to begin to make sense of this long list of systems types, in order to become more effective at choosing the kind of system that best fits a particular context. This requires putting systems thinking to use as an approach to understanding the nature of design itself, as was mentioned at the beginning of this chapter.

COMPLEX SYSTEMS

SIMPLE SYSTEMS (I.E., MECHANICAL, LINEAR, ETC.)

SPIRITUAL SYSTEMS

LIVING SYSTEMS

NATURAL SYSTEMS

ECOSYSTEMS

ABSTRACT SYSTEMS (E.G., NUMBERS, SYMBOLIC LOGIC ETC.)

ARTIFICIAL SYSTEMS

BELIEF SYSTEMS

WHOLE SYSTEMS

BIOLOGIC SYSTEMS

SOCIAL SYSTEMS

ORGANIZATIONAL SYSTEMS

INFORMATION SYSTEMS

EDUCATIONAL SYSTEMS

FUNCTIONAL SYSTEMS (E.G., TRANSPORTATION, HEALTH, ETC.)

MYTHIC SYSTEMS

PHILOSOPHIC SYSTEMS

Fig. 3-6 Illustration of Categories of Systems

A particular systems category does not generate an exclusive set of systems, but merely provides the continuum along which particular system concepts fall. Another way of stating this is that a systems category can identify the common ground within which each system concept falls. It is a matter of choice as to which set will be used to support the systems thinker, or practitioner, in his or her work.

The illustrations in the remainder of this chapter present ways to approach design through the means of systems based concepts; examples of systemic design aids that might be found in a designer's personal 'how to' design manual. We should note that the following examples are not meant to be used as *true* descriptors of systems designs, accurately explaining systems structure and behavior. Instead, they are pragmatic ways to communicate certain complex ideas and are merely design tools meant to assist in the ultimate design of more specific, custom-tailored designs from a systems perspective. They are examples of how a designer can form his or her design palette using a systems approach.

The categorization of systems is not restricted to a singular classification of logic. This is demonstrated below in the example of three conceivable categories of systems, based on the different logical divisions of social, scientific, or behavioral domains (see Fig. 3-7).

From a systems inquiry perspective, determining the category of a system is dependent on the tradition, or traditions, of inquiry used to describe and explain that particular system's concepts. For instance, a system or category of systems can be defined from a traditional scientific frame of reference, but it may also be explored using humanistic, artistic, technologic, spiritual, or other distinct traditions of inquiry. For example, a mythic system is designed from a spiritual tradition, while a school of art is designed from an artistic tradition. This implies that a system, including its category, can be defined or described using epistemological approaches that draw from a variety of designs of

101

inquiry. Now, what does this mean to the designer? It means that there are no true, fixed, or given types of systems or categories of systems, or even categories of elements making up a system. It means that determining a system's category is a matter of *perspective, intention* and *choice*.

SOCIAL SYSTEM CATEGORY

SPIRITUAL

CULTURAL

FAMILY

SOCIAL

SOCIO-TECHNICAL ORGANIZATION

SYSTEM SCIENCE CATEGORY

SOCIETIES

SPECIES

ORGANIC ASSEMBLIES

INORGANIC COMPOUNDS

SYSTEMS PRODUCTION CATEGORY

AUTOPOIETIC (SELF-MAKING)

ALOPOIETIC (OTHER-MAKING)

TELOPOIETIC (PURPOSE-MAKING)

MYTHOPOIETIC (MEANING-MAKING)

Fig. 3-7 Illustration of Types of Systems within Systemic Categories Formed within Social, Scientific and Production Domains

102

The work of one well-known systems philosopher, C. West Churchman, provides a good example. Churchman chose to explain systems from a people-centered perspective in which people are the dominant elements in his social systems category. He worked from an inclusive form of inquiry (a *compound*) that expanded the concept of systems science to include broader understandings of rational thinking than are commonly used (see Fig. 3-8).

CLIENT

PURPOSE OF SYSTEM

MEASURE OF PERFORMANCE OF SYSTEM

DECISION MAKER

BOUNDARY BETWEEN ENVIRONMENT AND SYSTEM

COMPONENTS OF SYSTEM

PLANNER

IMPLEMENTATION OF DESIGNS

GUARANTOR-OF-DESIGN SYSTEM

SYSTEMS PHILOSOPHER

SIGNIFICANCE OF SYSTEMS APPROACH

ENEMIES OF THE SYSTEMS APPROACH

Fig. 3-8 Churchman's Planning Categories with Focus on Human Agency

103

From his systems approach, he identified four categories of people who play essential roles in the activity of systems, including planning and design activities. These categories were further developed to include descriptions of role responsibilities and relationships (Churchman, 1979).

From this set of categories, Churchman developed a series of questions to investigate any situation (from a systems perspective) that was too complex and unstructured for standard problem solving approaches. His questions are in two parts. The first set of questions asks for an objective determination of the situation. The second set asks for a deontic determination (that which 'ought to be') of what should be taken into account including issues of ethics, equity and social justice. This is a mix of two traditions of inquiry—one objective and the other value-based.

The process of answering these questions provides a necessary first foothold in a complex, real-world situation. It allows the next steps to unfold with care. Those next steps include determining the make-up of the particular system's approach to inquiry and action in a way that will best serve that system's unique situation. This process is similar to that of the artist, who must choose the palette from which a painting will be created.

Such a systems approach not only integrates both objective and subjective thought processes, but also weaves in multiple traditions of inquiry as well. These forms of inquiry and action include: design and scientific, philosophic, artistic, humanistic, metaphysical, religious, professional, spiritual, pragmatic and technological traditions, and can help the designer build an overall systems approach to their particular design challenge.

All system inquiries are brought into focus by a particular frame of reference. This frame of reference is based on a set of categories and typologies. Whether a designer *formalizes* the categories of the systems he or she is working with, is up to them. It is a design decision, and therefore a matter of choice.

> Indeed, the selection of a definition of "systems" is a design choice, because throughout this essay it is the designer who is the chief figure. In other words, whether or not something is a system is regarded as a specific choice of the designer.

> C. West Churchman (1971)

As the designer begins to refine his or her other choices and develop categories and characterizations for individual systems, he or she is said to be *forming a palette of systems,* from which design judgments will then be made.

In a design process, a designer has to make judgments and decisions about how to approach reality. And, as we've said above, he or she will do this by selecting a mode of inquiry. Can he or she guarantee that the choices made are the absolute correct ones for the design in question? No. There is no way to discern what their choices might mean in the ultimate particular case of design. It will always be a choice that is at best based on *intention* and *will.* Most importantly, a designer must realize that all of these choices are *inevitable.* They cannot be avoided and therefore will be made whether the designer is aware he or she is making them, or not. A conscious approach is most definitely preferable. This requires the designer to acquire at least a working knowledge of different approaches from which to choose, as well as to devote considerable time to reflecting on the specifics of the present design situation and what is needed.

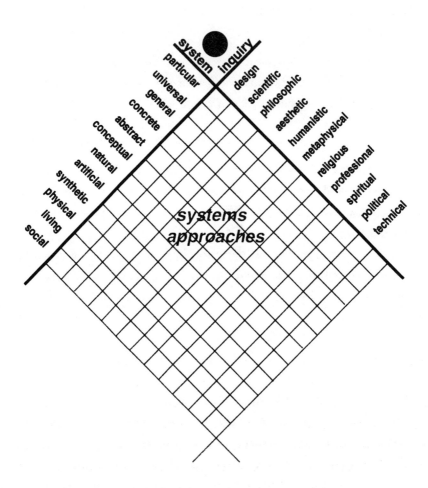

Fig. 3-9 An Example of a Systems Design Palette

Once specifically designed modes of inquiry are chosen, they are then brought into conjunction with the different types of systems (see Fig. 3-9) being studied. This becomes part of the development of a *palette for design*. Particularized relationships among various categories of systems—and these multiple modes of inquiry—create compounds of inquiry and action that assist in explaining or describing a specific complex system. They can also help to conceptualize such a system as a new design, when it does not yet exist. The capacity to create design palettes comprised of systems types in relationship to different designs of inquiry is essential for managing complex design projects.

The different types of systems listed on the left side of the matrix in Figure 3-9 collectively represent only one possible mix and are not meant to be a comprehensive inventory. Other systems types can be presented through alternative categories while maintaining the same category of types of inquiry as listed on the right side of the matrix. For instance, a category of *living systems* could include spiritual, cultural, social, organizational and organic dimensions. A category of *social systems* could include human, social, organizational, living, technical, natural, physical and socio-technical dimensions. These are just two systemic domains possible out of a large number of intentional choices. Any particular category of systemic types formulates a design palette, from which designers and others can combine the elements of their customized systems approach. The examples show how these conscious, or unconscious, choices of the design palette lead to concrete differences in ways to approach a design situation. This also implies that the chosen palette will inevitably lead to different outcomes of the design process.

It is quite possible to imagine how the two palette choices above will lead to very different descriptions and understandings of the same system. When a designer approaches the system at hand, with these two varying, conceptual tools, different things will be made visible and considered important. For instance, the category of social systems contains technical and socio-technical types of systems that the category of living systems does not. Thus, the social system category will more readily provide a basis for the inclusion of technologic issues. It is possible to perform a 'thought' experiment by applying different palettes to the same system. Such experiments will help the designer to develop an understanding of the ultimate meaning of alternative approaches.

An important aspect of systems design is systems *behavior*. Systems behavior is a combination of structure and process, or relationships and animation. Behavior is how a system acts over time within the constraints of its type of structure, functionality and purpose. Behavior is descriptive of both internal functional processes and externally directed activity. Externally directed behavior focuses on relationships with other systems, the system's environment or context. For instance, consider a category of systems types that includes the differentiation of complex, simple, dynamic and balanced.

By combining these systems types with internally and externally focused behaviors (such as designing, transforming, evolving, processing, changing and maintaining), a large number of design approaches are conceivable (see Fig. 3-10). For example, it is possible to think of a system that has the design competence to design other types of systems with different behavior from itself. It is also possible to conceptualize a system that has the design competence to engage in behavior focused on itself, such as in self-repair.

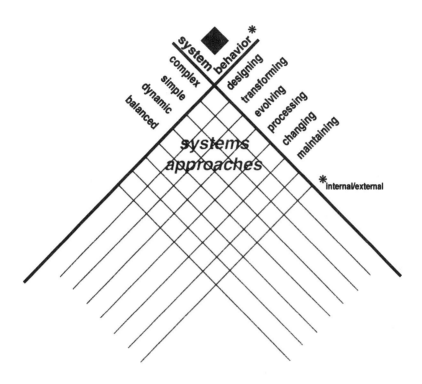

Fig. 3-10 Design Palette Consisting of Types of Systems and Systems Behavior

The category of types of behavior listed on the right side of the matrix in Figure 3-10 is just one possibility out of many. For example, systems behavior can be defined by types of reactions to environmental conditions, such as passive, reactive, adoptive, adaptive, evolutionary and intentional. Another example would be a category of behavior defined by the degrees of freedom that a system has within a teleological hierarchy, including controlled, deterministic, heuristic, purposive, purposeful, creative, phronesis based and design based.

Any particular combination of categories provides the means for conceptualizing a systemic approach to design that is most appropriate for a particular design situation.

As C. West Churchman points out (Churchman, 1971), conceptualizing a system is a matter of *design judgment*. Systems boundaries are determined as a matter of judgment as well. Just as an artist frames a painting, or a photographer crops a photo, a designer consciously selects those elements he or she believes to belong inside a given system. What relationships are to be established with other elements is also a matter of design judgment. Components, including subsystems, need to be interrelated (meaning in relationships, such as competition, cooperation, etc.). All systems can be placed within other systems, and every system is in relationship with an environment. Determining which components are part of a system, and which are parts of its environment, is yet another matter to be decided based on judgment. Every system is also within a context as a matter of *appreciative judgment* (see *Judgment* chapter).

Although not all systems types are useful in design, some are of fundamental importance. One such type defines systems by the degrees of freedom they have to form and direct their own behavior—i.e., the teleological levels open to ascertainment, versus those that are predetermined (see Fig. 3-11). Exploration into this class of systems has been advanced through the seminal work of Erik Jantsch (1975). This method of categorizing systems by teleological (or purpose-driven) behavior is important for a solid understanding of systems design. Why? Well, to begin with, any system that is being designed must have a certain, specific degree of freedom in order to function as intended (i.e., as specified through prescriptive design criteria). Second, it is important to make sure that *the designing system has*

110

at least one degree of freedom more than the system being designed. The carpet does not fabricate the weaver; the pot does not form the potter.

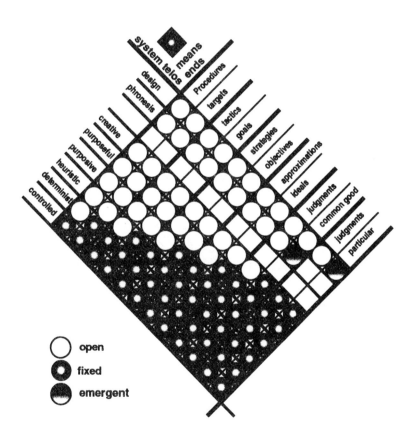

Fig. 3-11 Systems Defined by Degrees of Freedom

The designer must have more freedom than that which he or she is designing. For example, an organizational design function in a corporation cannot have equal, or lower levels of, authority (degrees of freedom) than that part of the organization it is designing. If the organization itself is being designed, then the designing system must include individuals who can exceed the degrees of freedom inherent in the internal roles of authority of that organization. This defines, in part, the meaning of leadership from a whole systems design perspective.

A common mistake in systems design, especially organizational systems design, is to assume that there are universally ideal systems. That one size can fit all, so to speak. In reality, this is never the case. No matter how common the circumstance of a design situation, it is always necessary to carefully consider and specify what degrees of freedom (or teleological behavior) a system needs, in relation to the intended purpose of the design. For example, an organizational system that is designed to manage a nuclear power station should not have high degrees of freedom designed into it. It is essential to have its behavior limited because of safety and risk factors. Therefore, this organizational system must behave in very deterministic ways. There is no need, or desire, for creative behavior, or surprises, from this type of system. On the other hand, airline pilots need to have greater degrees of freedom, given that their flying conditions can change dramatically on any given flight. They must have the freedom to respond, using their *navigational* judgment, to surprising situations as they occur.

A system that is itself capable of design requires the highest degree of freedom of all. Such a design-capable system is a compound of its necessary degrees of freedom and the traditions of inquiry that form the epistemological foundation from which the system's designing activities will be approached (see Fig. 3-12). A concept center, innovation center, design studio or 'skunk works' within a corporation, that is charged with coming up with new and creative ideas, can only create systems that have fewer degrees of freedom than those represented by team members in the design team.

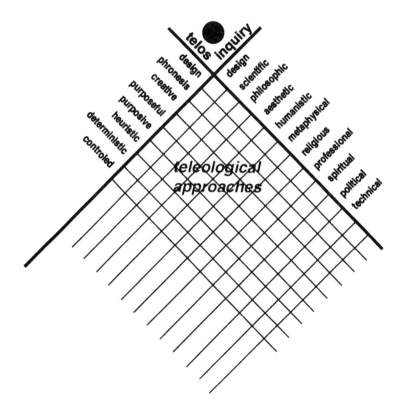

Fig. 3-12 Palette for the Design of Design Inquiry

If a new design for the entire organization is needed, then that means the top-level executive, the one with the maximum degrees of freedom in the corporation, must be a member of the design team. This maximization of degrees of freedom forms the design palette for the designing of an inquiring system, in this case, a *design inquiry* system. This design inquiry system, or process, is the kind of world-approach that a design approach attempts to present and emulate.

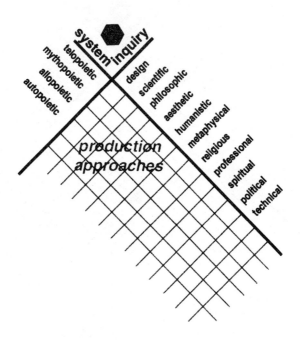

Fig. 3-13 Example of a Design Palette for Production

An essential aspect of design, in addition to its process of inquiry, is its capacity to produce what has been formed as a design concept. An example of a palette for *design production* (see Fig. 3-13) would include categories of the capacity 'to make'. *Poiesis*, a Greek term for 'making', forms the basic root word for what we define as varieties of the capacity 'to make'.

Systems that have the capacity for self-production, or *self-making*, are called *autopoietic*. Those that have the ability to make *for* and *with* others are designated as *allopoietic*. From a design tradition, systems that make meaning can be classified as *mythopoietic*. Those that have the capacity to create purpose can be classified as *telopoietic*. These categories of 'making' constitute examples of the types of design approaches that should be considered as one ponders the variety of options available in the production phase of design.

As we examine the nature of design and designing, it becomes increasingly clear why *systems thinking is the organizing element in design reasoning*. Systems, as objectified things (whether concrete or abstract), provide us the necessary context and focus for design activity. Also, design palettes are essentially formed using a systems approach to choice and judgment. As every design is part of an environmental system, formed by a systemic context that carries systemic conse-quences with its implementation, the best design is one that is a whole systems design.

Systems thinking is a necessary component of design. Indeed, design inquiry is, in effect, simply a particular type of systems approach, which espouses a specific worldview and world-approach.

4. THE WHOLE

What do we mean when we say that a design constitutes a *whole*? What does it mean to design *holistically*? The term whole and derivative forms—like holism and holistic—are used in diverse ways. The term whole is often taken to mean the entirety of existence, an all-inclusive perspective. The term whole is also understood, utilizing the spiritual concept of oneness, that all things are merely glimpsed reflections of a unitary reality. A permutation of this is the understanding that all things are connected or interconnected systemically. Whole can also mean the complete or comprehensive collection of things, whether abstract or concrete. From a design perspective, the concepts of emergence and composition are illustrative of what is meant by whole or holistic.

One of the foundations of design is its holistic character. A design never exists in isolation. It is always part of a larger whole and is itself whole. In design, when we say that something is a 'whole', it means that it is a complex ensemble of *compound, meaning* and *presence* (see Fig. 4-1). Let us take a look at these elements of wholeness. A *compound* is a blend of material and substance. It is the *stuff* of which things are made not the *form* of things. Drawing on an example from the last chapter, the compound known as water is stuff made up of hydrogen and oxygen. Its forms, on the other hand, can be seen in such things as the ocean's surf or in a crystalline snowflake. *Meaning* is revealed to us through the ordering potential of systemic relationships that have been created intentionally, in response to purpose, in fulfillment of an end. Now, what are we saying here? We're saying those unifying forces

117

which cause things to stand together, in ordered form, provide a comprehensible unity of significance, importance and value, thus creating meaning for those individuals who are part of the whole or closely related to the whole. *Presence*, the third ingredient in the rich mixture that constitutes wholeness, is the emergent essence of the whole. This essence is brought into reality, conceptually or perceptually, through different levels of apprehension, including *appearance, character* and *soul*.

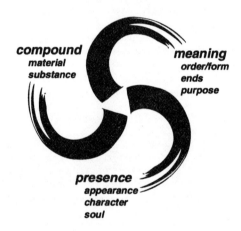

Fig. 4-1 Dimensions of Whole

When a holistic approach is employed by a designer, he or she must be careful not to disaggregate, compartmentalize, polarize, or ignore attributes of undifferentiated life experiences. Traditional distinctions that deny integration, such as mind and body, science and art, reason and imagination, are examples of non-holistic approaches that represent popular, intellectual habits of mind. It's hard to break the scientific habit of dividing things into distinct parts, with distinct,

118

categorical differences. For example, in the process of developing and presenting ideas that are foundational to the design of this book, we were continually challenged to remain inclusive, relational and contextual. We found it difficult to hold things together in unity and not to be drawn too deeply into a focus that landed primarily on distinctions and divisive separations. It was through the principle of holism that we were able to capture our initial intention.

Although it's true that "the whole is greater than the sum of its parts," we must also acknowledge that the whole *is of* those parts. This idea has important consequences. Namely, you cannot design a whole, without taking into consideration the selection of parts available. You cannot conceptually (or concretely) impose a whole onto parts. It is not possible to design a whole, and impose that emergent quality onto parts that do not embody the whole *a priori*. The whole takes its essence from the nature of its parts. There is an inseparable relationship between the parts and the whole. We also need to remember that a whole is always part of something more comprehensive—another whole. This means that a whole—made up of parts interacting as a system, functioning to serve a particular end—invariably will become the means for an even greater end.

It is not uncommon for the concept of 'vision' to be used as representative of a whole. But this can lead to confusion in relationship to design. A vision is not the manifestation of a whole, an outcome of the process of composition. A whole can never be fully described before it is composed, even with the parts at hand. It is not possible to impose a predetermined vision of wholeness onto parts, in order to obtain a specific whole as an outcome. To create wholes, it is necessary to compose them from particular elements—elements that are then destined to lose their individual identity to a transcendent

119

identity. Early definitions of holism were concerned with this relationship of parts and wholes.

> Holism shows these opposites as reconciled and harmonized in
> the whole. It shows whole and parts as aspects of each other.

Encyclopaedia Britannica (1927)

As shown by the variety of definitions employed in contemporary
philosophies and theories of holism or holistic approaches—there is
no standard understanding of holism. Some of the most common
concepts share the trait of 'claimed comprehensiveness'. The term
whole is often used to imply an inclusive understanding of the
relationship of everything to everything. This definition arises from the
scientific approach to the concept, where 'wholes' are defined as the
study of comprehensive systems. The underlying assumption is that
you need to know everything about a phenomenon in order to understand it. It also implies that everything is connected to everything,
leaving no natural boundaries. This comprehensiveness requires that
everything with a relationship to the phenomenon of interest is
included in its analysis. Luckily, holism can be viewed from a variety
of other angles.

One such perspective defines the whole as a comprehensive
understanding of the world in metaphysical terms, such as spirituality
and mysticism. In this case, the belief is that there is a whole from
which everything emerges. Sometimes, this is expanded to include the
concept that each and every thing in the world is a holograph of the
metaphysical whole, reflecting the whole at every resolution of detail.
Like the scientific approach to holism, this understanding of holism
treats the concept of complete knowledge as the ideal.

120

These scientific and metaphysical approaches to holism are manifested to varying degrees in various contemporary schools of thought, including deep ecology, Gaia theory, the theory of implicate order and the New Age sciences. These movements advocate a belief in the holistic character of reality, and advocate that this belief should become the first, and sometimes only, ordering principle for change. These definitions of holism are stimulating and important antidotes to the overpowering habits of reductive analysis, but they are not fertile ground from which to develop design principles. From a design perspective, the 'whole' is not something merely to adapt to or emulate.

Another definition of holism comes from the perspective of a systems approach, where the concept of *emergence* is a seminal attribute. As indicated earlier, a commonly stated belief in systems thinking is that the whole is greater than the sum of its parts. This means that there are emergent qualities of a whole that can only be revealed as transcendent properties, different from those properties displayed by the individual and separate parts of the whole. This perspective of whole introduces a concept that provides an important insight that leads to a deeper understanding of design.

What do we mean by an emergent quality? In design terms (as discussed in the *Systems* chapter), we are talking about a deterministic outcome that is the necessary consequence of the relationships, interactions and collective behavior of the constituent parts or elements of an integrated system. For example, this could be something as simple as the aggregate action of a flock of birds or school of fish that is perceived as a distinct and unified behavior pattern (i.e., 'flocking' and 'schooling'). It can also be something as complex as someone's personality that is apprehended as a unified expression of an

121

individual's character. Or, it can simply be the essence of a work of art.

Emergence can be either a predictable outcome or an unpredictable outcome of holistic constructs. The concept of an unpredictable, emergent quality highlights the role of chance in natural wholes—while the predictable highlights the role of necessity. Emergence can also be expected as an outcome of intentionality in designed wholes. Emergence embodies not only an aggregation of the collective elements of a system, but also the qualities of the underlying structure of the system. In this light, emergent qualities can be understood as *general* qualities, brought into existence by the way a whole is bound together by substance and order.

Another way of defining wholes, and one that is a foundation of design, is the characterization of the whole as a *composition*. This definition applies to both natural and designed wholes (see Fig. 4-2). Natural compositions are defined by the emergent qualities of contingent (i.e., depends on circumstances), or universal (i.e., without condition or exception), wholes. In contrast, designed compositions are *ultimate particular wholes*, thus unique and singular. This type of whole is evoked through intentional acts of composition, undertaken for specific purposes, at a particular time and place.

Natural wholes can be defined as having attributes such as being comprehensive, necessary, emergent and viable, plus they have a presence in the world and an influence upon it. The properties of designed wholes are equivalent, but different in kind, in contrast to natural wholes. For example, in the case of a designed whole, the attribute of being *adequate* replaces the attribute of being *comprehensive*.

122

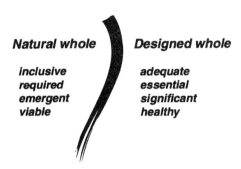

Fig. 4-2 Whole as Composition

A natural system is comprehensive from the perspective of what is true about it. Its comprehensiveness can never be fully disclosed because of its complexity. A designed system is adequate because it is only as complex and comprehensive as it needs to be in order to fulfill its intended purpose. Relatively speaking, its complexity is comprehensible because it is the product of human intention. In similar fashion, designed whole attributes, such as *essential, significant* and *healthy* (for living systems), stand as counterparts to the relevant attributes of natural wholes. *These attributes of designed wholes become guides for the intentional composition of wholes.* These guiding qualities are relevant, both in relation to the process of composition and to the designed outcome.

Often, readers are more familiar with the designed whole attributes of *health* expressed in terms of aesthetics and ethics, than they are with the first three that we listed—adequate, essential and significant. Unfortunately, in contemporary processes of designing, the holistic attributes of the adequate, essential and significant are too often substituted by criteria that lack the same depth of meaning. The adequate is generally substituted by the attribute of *more*, the essential by *faster* and significant by the *quick fix*, or short-term gain.

The most elusive and unfamiliar concept in design—from a holistic perspective—may be the idea of the *adequate*. This concept can be difficult to understand, given the unquestioned assumption that any plan for action must be grounded in *comprehensive* analysis. It is an article of faith, left over from the days when being comprehensive was believed to be, not only possible, but also necessary. In the age of enlightenment, the abiding faith of the Encyclopedists was that all that was worth knowing could be known. Their faith also held that this knowledge could be brought to bear on any situation, thus providing a clear, accurate description and explanation of the situation at hand, thereby illuminating right decisions. This hypostasis has become the benchmark upon which professional decision-making rests to this day.

For designers, there are two problems with this belief. The first problem is that design choices may be *based on* reason, but they are not *made by* reason. That is, design draws on rational thinking (e.g., the systems approach, disciplinary thinking and the scientific method), but it is not merely a rationalized, logical process. It is a process that includes imagination, intuition, feeling and emotion as well. The second problem is that the explosion of information in the past century has made it impossible to be comprehensive about anything. Those who continue to cling to the belief that comprehensibility can be achieved will invariably experience analysis paralysis.

Design is often assumed to lie comfortably in the shade of the 'comprehensive decision-making' umbrella, because it is frequently understood to be primarily about making something concrete, or planning for something specific, or simply making something aestheti-cally pleasing. Although these are common features in traditional

124

physical design, there is actually much more to design than what these features would imply. One of modern design's key distinctions is that design decisions are made as design judgments, leading to the creation of something that did not exist before. And, it is an inescapable fact that these crucial design judgments are always made within a context of the *adequate* rather than the comprehensive.

Every design process unfolds within a unique situation: a complex and dynamic reality. A designer always acts in response to that reality. We do not have unlimited freedom, resources, information, or time. We can never achieve absolute perfection in design, or any other domain of human existence for that matter. Rather, we embrace the adequate. By adequate, we do not mean the mediocre. This is not about dampening a designer's ambition and passion. Instead, we use the term 'adequate' as simply a way of framing the real nature of design.

Design is not the pursuit of an ideal concept. It is not the creation of an ultimate vision, in a perfectible world, where everything, including sufficient information, authority and resources, is in the hands of the designer. On the contrary, design can only be fully actualized by all the circumstances and specifics that make a design situation uniquely particular. We are not trumpeting compromise, or surrender, to the imperfections, shortcomings and incompleteness of each unique situation. Instead, we are asking you to explore the splendor of the possible, to create something *not-yet-existing*, based on the fragile realities of each unique situation, and encompassing the desires of real individuals.

> But compromise too is temporary and futile. It usually means
> merely a postponement of the issue. The truth does not lie

125

"between" the two sides. We must be ever on our guard against sham reconciliation...

...integration might be considered a qualitative adjustment, compromise a quantitative one. In the former there is a change in the ideas and their action tendencies; in the latter there is mere barter of opposed "rights of way."

M. P. Follett (1930)

It is important to appreciate the danger of creating a design motivated by a quest for the ideal design solution. This often leads to the creation of something that cannot be supported, maintained, afforded, or controlled by the beneficiaries of the design. Perfectly glorious designs can bring ruin, or the threat of ruin, because they are not formed in the context of the adequate, but formed by the unrealized quest for the comprehensive. Therefore, establishing a firm grasp of the adequate may be the most difficult and important judgment made in a design process. This judgment will, in turn, have impact on all other design judgments in the process.

The adequate can also be understood as an emergent quality evoked through judgments of composition that bring together things of very different or diverse natures to form a meaningful whole. A designer's judgment is used to mediate among such differences using compositional principles like proportion, measure, balance, contrast and complementarity. Mediation in this case means the ability to judge the *mean* in the Aristotelian sense rather than a determination of an arithmetic average, utilitarian trade-off or political compromise. The quality of mediated difference is exemplified by examining the challenge of creating a holistic composition out of the distinctive

126

differences between justice and compassion, tradition and innovation, creativity and control, or stability and change. These are all examples of concepts that are valuable in themselves, but that become even more valuable when combined in a composition of mediated wholeness. For example, justice and compassion emerge as mercy, a holistic quality. Other examples can be as simple as the obvious functional difference between a hammer and a chisel that, when mediated with skill and good judgment, result in a great work of art. Compositional judgments that combine functional differences of this type do not result in reconciliation, resolution or trade-off, but in an adequate composition. It also does not result in an ideal, or absolute, design. Compositions are never the result of a recipe or rule. Rather, they are an outcome of judgment. The essential value of each difference is enhanced and enriched, by being brought into a particular, compositional relationship that adequately facilitates the desired outcome of an emergent design.

Getting back to our initial list of designed whole attributes, we would like to spend a little time examining that which is *essential* in design. By *essential*, we are referring to discernment, and the inclusion of anything that is judged to be an intentional necessity to the design, in order to fulfill authentic human needs and desires. This would include all desiderata at both the particular and collective level. Often, there is a sense that something important is missing in a design, something that not only frustrates its function, but blocks its service capacity as well. The thing that is missing is an essential attribute.

A third attribute of designed wholes is the *significant*, which deals with meaning making. Designed wholes are created by intention, to evoke emergent forms and behaviors that embody the essence of human potential more fully. Some of what we assume to be a natural

127

element of our humanity is in actuality the consequence of a design originally. For example, human 'rights' are the outcome of historical social system designs.

These three attributes of the designed whole—the adequate, the significant and the essential—can be used for two purposes. They can guide intentional compositions of designed wholes, or they can act as a foundation for a critique of designed wholes. A designer needs to have the skill of discernment, a sensibility for proportions, which is essential to compositional mediation, and competence in judgment making to actively compose wholes with these attributes.

One way to acquire these skills is to examine and critique existing designs. By critiquing different types of designs, from the perspective of wholes, a designer can begin to acquire a sense of the designs work as wholes and those that do not (this is further discussed in the chapter *The Splendor of Design*).

It is also possible to expand this critique to a broader class of wholes. If the adequate, the significant and the essential are attributes for the real, then there are corresponding attributes for the true and the ideal (see Fig. 4-3).

With these attributes in mind, it is possible to make an evaluation of all sorts of wholes. Such an exercise might help a designer to better understand what distinguishes a designed whole from other types of wholes. These attributes are not exclusive—a wise designer does not dispense with the attributes of the ideal, or the true. In fact, he or she has to act within all three perspectives, never forgetting that the outcome of a holistic design process is a designed whole. In order to assure that a design process is robust and adequate, it is essential that it is a compound of the real, true and ideal.

frames of reference	design evaluation attributes
real	*adequate* *significant* *essential*
true	*efficient* *aesthetic* *ethical*
ideal	*ultimate truth* *perfect beauty* *absolute good*

Fig. 4-3 Critique of Wholes

Some attributes, such as efficiency, are easier to evaluate than others, as they have a tradition, in our culture, of being measured and critiqued. The most difficult attributes to evaluate are those associated with the real because they are unique and particular.

These attributes have a quality that, by necessity, brings the designer into a mode of service that demands a higher level of empathy and communication, with all those to be benefited by the design. Also, the attributes are relational and incommensurable, and therefore cannot be measured by some general *standard*.

The idea of whole is commonly related to the combined notion of comprehensiveness and scale. Everything is believed to be tightly connected to everything and thus must include everything. But the notion of the whole applies not only to large comprehensive designs, which by their size or impact make them natural to consider as

129

wholes, but also to small designed artifacts and processes. Thinking in terms of wholes is important for every design no matter the scale or consequence. In fact, the degree to which each design is experienced as a whole is determined solely by the judgment of the designer. Therefore, the notion of the whole is a foundational property of intentional design.

III. FUNDAMENTALS

The design approach requires us to acquire a certain number of fundamental skills. These activities make up the palette that sustains and nourishes design inquiry and action. Although you will be able to intellectually understand these approaches, you will never be able to learn them abstractly. Fundamentals for a design approach are an open-and-shut case of 'learning by doing'. They require continuous practice. In effect, they are acquired in the same manner that fundamentals for sports, art, or music are learned. Mastery of these fundamentals is not an end to be reached, but an exciting, ongoing process. Accomplishment is measured in terms of excellence and quality.

The fundamentals of design thinking include: *desiderata, interpretation and measurement, imagination and communication, judgment, composition and production, and care taking.*

5. DESIDERATA

Change in our world can be initiated in basically two ways. We can act because we want to move away from a situation we do not like, or we can act towards an imagined and desired situation.

To often, the good intentions that arise from the recognition of a need for change lead to paralysis. Now, what do we mean by this? We mean that agents of change are often paralyzed by the very reality of their situation. This is because the strategies for change, to which most of us commonly default, lead to dead-ends, rather than next-best steps. Some of these dead-ends include analysis paralysis, wicked problem paralysis, value paralysis and holistic paralysis (i.e., attempting to be comprehensive). Analysis paralysis occurs when too much divergent information is generated, without any effective means for convergence. The paralyzing effect of confronting wicked problems, rather than tame problems, comes from bumping up against the limits of rationality itself (see *Systems* chapter). Value paralysis occurs when any and every value system is taken into account without any means of transcending the differences and diversity. The paralysis of holism occurs when there are no automatic means for bounding or limiting comprehensive expansion.

This unfortunate situation exists because all of these strategies have a common foundation in 'problem solving'. Their focus is on only *that-which-is* (description and explanation), versus *that-which-ought-to-be* (ethics and morality), without consideration for *that-which-is-desired* (desiderata).

Now, we can, and do, cause actions which lead to change in the world. Some of these actions are based on *that-which-is*, because we believe in a true, logically structured reality; one based on natural laws. We hold fast to a reality that can be understood through science and changed by technology. For most of us, the world is thought of as a given, already finished as a design, and we are put on earth to react and respond to this design. Even in post-modern thinking, which recognizes the temporary stature of natural laws and the relativity of anything in the category of truth—particularly social truth—it is believed that change is based on stabilized, universal principles of cause and effect.

However, there is a missing insight in this view of reality, which is, description and explanation (i.e., science) do not prescribe action, nor do prediction and control (i.e., technology) justify action. Around the world, billions of dollars are spent on studies and projects based on science and technology. This is done in the belief that by rubbing the two together the spark of prescriptive action will be given off. Unfortunately, this never happens, because the spark must come from a different source.

It is also important to note that we can, and do, cause changes based on *that-which-ought-to-be*—because this, too, is believed to be a kind of truth. It is truth that is logically formed and based on ethical laws, religious precepts and moral codes. Yet, our actions in this case always stem from a reactive mode. The trigger for this cause of action is anything between an uneasy sense of ethical transgression to moral outrage. The outcome is as diverse as good works and holy wars.

We also create changes based on what we want, including *that-which-can-be*, as demonstrated by our emphasis on technologic innovations. We can create everything from biological clones to

134

smaller, faster, more complex electronic devices. Because we have the ability to create them, we then become convinced we want them, and that they are needed. Yet, even though what we want is most often driven by our immediate short-term needs and interests, there is always a deeper, more profound sense of want, which is expressed in the aesthetic terms of values. This deep sense of wanting occurs even without a belief in natural order.

These three approaches to intentional change have the following correspondence. What we *want* can be seen as our aesthetics. What we believe *ought to be* relates to our ethics. What *is* corresponds to reason. In any particular situation, however, there is never just one approach present. Depending on what we perceive as the basis for intentional action, there will be different proportions among the three, aesthetics, ethics and reason. In real-world contexts, everything is a blend.

In this book, we use the concept of *desiderata* (i.e., desires) as an inclusive whole. That is, we see it as a concept that includes all three of the following approaches: aesthetics, ethics and reason. But, within this concept, the aggregated effect of these three approaches transcends their summation, forming an emergent quality that is characteristic of compositions, or wholes. Desiderata are about what we intend the world to be, and is the *integrative outcome of all three approaches in concert.* It is the escape route from the strategies for change, which box us into paralysis, blind action, or slavish mimicry (see Fig. 5-1). Desiderata are the *voice* of design.

When there is a call for change in society, people generally use one of two typical strategies to take action: the 'sweep-in' approach and the 'block-out' approach. Sweep-in approaches are characterized by an ambition to rush in and discover the right solution to the problem, by

135

applying a comprehensive examination of the needs in question. This type of approach often leads to analysis paralysis as a consequence.

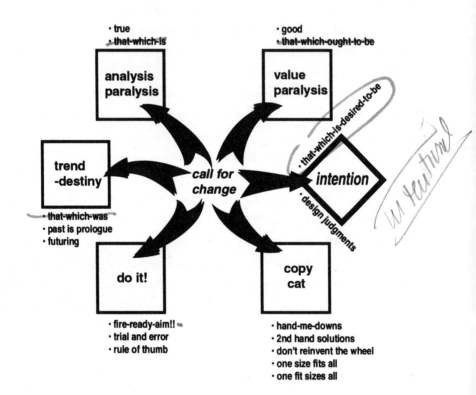

Fig. 5-1 Default Options and the Intentional Option for Change

People become paralyzed because they are confronted with too much information—while at the same time they feel they have a need for even more information. Comprehensive, rational analysis creates more questions than are answered. Rather than converging on an optimal

136

design solution, the process diverges endlessly into greater and greater numbers of details.

On the other hand, block-out approaches try to use simple, often ready-made strategies to make decisions, without investing the time and energy on in-depth examinations. Every significant design situation is complex and unique. Design solutions that have been created for other complex, unique situations do not match the particular situation at hand. In addition, generalized solutions that fit all or most situations are course and grossly formed. They do not have the complexity and refinement of detail sufficient to match the richness of a unique design situation. This does not mean that designs must be complicated, or expensive, or excessive in any other way as a consequence. The best design for a situation may be elegantly simple and economic, while at the same time being the most appropriate response to the unique requirements of the design situation. For example, when a global or national policy is applied to particular populations of people, in particular places, at particular times, it is often disastrous. To illustrate, an educational policy may work for one school, or set of similar schools, while being ineffective, or worse, ruinous, to a diversity of schools in the same administrative jurisdiction.

Clearly, neither of these options is ideal when confronted with a call for change. A more satisfying and rewarding path requires one to engage in an *intentional design approach*, based on a careful examination of desiderata guided by design judgment (see Fig. 5-1).

Now, how does one start down this road? How do we use a design approach to assess and respond to a call for change? To begin with, a *needs assessment* may be necessary but is insufficient alone. Too often, this is the initial, inadequate step in approaches to intentional change. More appropriate for a design approach is a *desiderata assessment*.

137

Determining needs is a responsible activity for any agent of change to engage in on behalf of those who are in need of help. However, for those wanting to be served, it is essential to assess desires. This is particularly true when the change involves the creation, or modification, of new social structures, such as business organizations, governmental agencies or social institutions.

It is important to note that *assessing* need is very different from *creating* need. The latter, is a common approach to change, but decidedly more suspect—especially when focused on the creation of new technologies, commodities and services. Taken too far, this approach can lead to over-consumption, addictions and self-destructive behavior, as demonstrated by the tobacco industry. Most recently, technology has also been considered 'addictive' and 'self-destructive'. For example, the artifacts of advanced technology, especially computer technology, including computer games and the World Wide Web, have been criticized for the negative effect they may be having on human beings concomitant with the benefits they promise.

The aggressive and manipulative character of advertising and marketing, when focused on creating need, has been successful in shaping markets for products and technologies that people did not contract for out of desire, but which they have been successfully coerced into adapting. Similarly, the tradition of science has also been used as a justification for creating need. The motto of the 1933 Chicago World's Fair, as Donald Norman (1993) reminds us, was: "Science Finds, Industry Applies, Man Conforms." Scientific break-throughs and the resultant applied technologies are treated as predestined realities for humans. A typical response to questions of

138

what the future may look like is: "The technology is there, it will happen!" It is considered to be a matter of 'trend destiny'.

A created need is an imposed desire. It is a *faux desire,* which originates outside of the individual's own generative nature. It is preformed and impressed upon a person in their role as consumer or end user, through persuasion and manipulation. Still, when moderated, the creation of need can, and does, act as the engine for an effective free market system, with all its benefits and successes. It is also important to remember that the creative work of artists and innovators creates new expectations or needs, as people encounter the new and unexpected creations of individual expression.

At this juncture, we want to emphasize that with any of the above approaches, there are problems with focusing too heavily on need as the key human motivation for change or innovation. Need implies that the desired situation is clearly understood, and that the real state of affairs, which is also clearly understood, is an undesired one. The difference between the desired state and the actual state is framed as the problem. It is also assumed that there is no difficulty in determining the needs that must be satisfied in order to realize the desired state. It is assumed that the process of satisfying needs can be efficiently accomplished through a rational and direct problem solving approach.

However, focusing strictly on our needs has allowed the fields of our desires to go fallow. Our understanding of motivation, triggered by what we desire (i.e., desiderata assessment), as opposed to what we need, remains remarkably undeveloped. *Human intention, when motivated by desiderata other than need, reshapes the entire process for intentional change.* To be intentional from a deep understanding of *that-which-is-desired,* rather than from a difference between *that-which-is* and *that-which-needs-to-be,*

139

reverses the assumption about what can be known from the beginning. A needs-based change, animated through a problem solving approach, assumes that the appropriate outcome is known from the start.

In this frame of reference, when people speak of 'vision' it is as a preformed image, whereas a desire-based change process leads to a desired outcome but does not start with that outcome already neatly in place. Needs-based design is founded on the erroneous assumption that a need or problem is easily discerned. The reality of course is that needs are not clearly discerned at all. What do people really *need* beyond the needs of basic survival? People in the developing regions of the world live with much less than people in developed economies feel they 'need'.

People desire to flourish and not just survive. They may not need music or art to survive, but they certainly desire them both. A need is a base-line condition that must be mitigated in order to support and stabilize a given situation. The hungry need to be fed and the cold need to be sheltered—but people desire to be more than 'needy' creatures. Desire is the destabilizing trigger for transformational change, which facilitates the emergence of new possibilities and realizations of human 'being'.

In today's world, the newspapers are filled with reports of action that came from a reactive need for change. Regardless of whether it stems from business, political, or personal affairs, change emerges out of negative responses to events, or situations in the world. The justification for action arises out of what we fear, what makes us angry, what hurts us, what we hate, or what is humiliating us. Politicians in democracies around the world demonstrate leadership by identifying which, of the many things that threaten us, ought to be dealt with, in

140

which order and in what way. Voters participate by identifying all their own reactive issues—scared into action against threats both real and imagined.

These reactive responses lock us into an understanding of the world through the filter of problem solving. Russell Ackoff (1978) has pointed out that getting away from what we *don't* want, does not guarantee that we get what we *do* want. On one level we inherently understand this. We know that if we back away from danger, we might back into an even more dangerous situation. Still, everyday conversations are filled with the language of problems, problem recognition and problem solution. But as we've intimated earlier, rather than allowing our various problems to run our lives, we would be wise to approach the world from a design perspective and engage our desiderata in our approach to intentional change.

As stated earlier, the term, desiderata, refers to those things that are desired. Desiderata can be expressed through three distinct domains: the mind's desire, the heart's desire and the soul's desire. A desideratum is something that is roused out of a want, a desire, a hope, a wish, a passion, an aspiration, an ambition, a quest, a call to, a hunger for, or will towards.

In our culture, desires are often treated as low-level needs—things that we wish for but could live without. But desiderata are not a response to the problem of an unfulfilled human need. The negative impulse towards action, which arises out of such a felt need, is completely different from the positive impulse born out of the desire to create situations, systems of organization, or concrete artifacts which enhance our life experience. Rather than treating the source of these aspirations as needs, we believe it is helpful to refer to them as design intentions.

141

Desire can be understood as the 'force' that provides us with intrinsic guidance and energy. Desires constitute that which we long for. As humans, we use our desires as a way to understand how we can fulfill our lives. But desires are not all good. To find out what we desire, we have to name them, reflect upon them and examine them. When we examine our desires, we often find the bag fairly well mixed; with both the good and the bad. It is necessary in this process to accept both types of desires. Over time, we learn to discipline the negative desires and live out the positive ones. To differentiate positive desires from negative ones is one of our lifelong tasks as human beings. Rosaleen Trainor (2001) has called this process 'befriending our desires'. She explains that when we become aware of, and comfortable with, our desires, they begin to have an accepted place in our lives and can function as a form of guidance. In effect, they help us form our intentions.

Let's take a look at an example of a desideratum that functions as a guide. The desire for love is universal, but it is experienced differently, depending on the particular design of inquiry and action we choose (see Fig. 5-2). In the real, love takes on the form of *eros*—love of the physical world. In the true, love is manifested as *agape*—an abstracted form of social love. And, in the ideal, love is elevated to *philo*—an unconditional love of the ultimate.

This example of love, as a particular type of desideratum, seen through the lenses of three different forms of intentionality, demonstrates the symbiotic relationship between desiderata and intention. In a philosopher's sense, intentionality is much more than just intending to do something. It means any way that the mind has of referring to objects and states of affairs in the world (Searle, 1983). As Searle points out, it is one of the two basic states of mind, consciousness and

142

intentionality. Furthermore, he argues that intentionality, itself, is two-pronged, consisting of belief and desire. It is at this level of resolution, within the very big idea of intentionality, that the concept of design intention, as an expression of that desire, is developed.

Designs of Inquiry & Action

Desideratum	the real	the true	the ideal
love	eros	agape	philo

Fig. 5-2 A Desideratum Expressed through Three Forms of Intention

One of the key concepts concerning intention arose in the philosophic discourse of the Middle Ages. At that time, the idea of aim, as in aiming an arrow, became central to the unfolding meaning of intention. That is, that intention is not the target, nor the purpose, nor an end state, but is principally the *process of giving direction*. This distinction is an important one for design, because it is this judgment of intention that ultimately determines what strategy of inquiry and action will be used in any particular situation.

The form of action decided on affects the concomitant modes of inquiry associated with it. These systems of intention are often referred to as cultures of inquiry and action, and are defined in terms of academic categories, such as: design, science, art, the humanities, spirituality and technology (Snow, 1959). Although each culture can be inclusive of the others, there is a distinct aim for each which is directed away from the others. Some of the intellectual traditions, born from these cultures, include: creativity, innovation, research, management and problem solving. As in social cultures, different combinations of traditions live within different cultures of intention. For example, science at its best is inclusive of both creativity and objectivity. The humanities are inclusive of scientific research, rational problem solving and individual innovation. Design is inclusive of creativity and innovation, applied research and project management.

The intentional approaches associated with design also happen to be fundamental to the development and application of good leadership. This is no accident. Leaders require many approaches and skills to wisely guide their followers. One of the most important, yet most undeveloped, is design. Two terms often define good leadership; these terms are character and vision. The need for vision dominates almost any discussion of leadership today. Leaders are expected to have a vision, around which followers can rally and towards which they can surge. Vision becomes something that is given, a solution to a problem. Strategic planning, and similar methods for the management of change, have grown out of the belief that vision, and visionary leadership, are *a priori* factors in any intentional change process.

On the other hand, intention is best understood, not as a vision, but as the aiming and subsequent emergence of a desired outcome (see Fig. 5-3). Desiderata help to aim and form one's intentions. Unlike a vision, *the outcome is not there when the process begins.* The outcome only emerges based on the situation, desiderata and intention. This process is very different from many common approaches, where action is seen as a consequence of a defined goal. Now, in any intentional process, we know that we can easily produce goals that would be closer to our desires than the present. But intention is not

144

only about where to go, it is also about how to get there—how to aim so as to move closer to our desires.

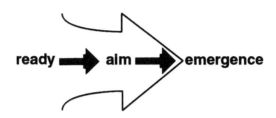

Fig. 5-3 Intention as Aiming

Within the Zen tradition, a deep understanding of intention, as a process of aiming, has been developed. In the classic book *Zen in the Art of Archery*, Herrigel (1953) shows how the notion of aiming can be developed by careful attention and by letting go of our everyday assumptions on how to reach our goals.

The process of aiming (intention) can be expanded upon by elaborating on the conceptual context, within which intentionality takes place. In the case of design intention, vision is the outcome of a process triggered by desiderata that is framed and contained by appreciative judgment (distinguishing foreground from background). It is animated by motivation and intensified through the alignment of design behaviors among participants (see Fig. 5-4). The design insights that are revealed as a consequence of the above encountering the "mysterium tremendum" (the great mystery of the human condition) emerge as an intense, but undifferentiated, seed of wisdom, known as a *parti* (the idea of *parti* is further developed in the chapter *Composition*.)

Through the design team's energy and focus, the parti is developed into an equivalent image, from which vision is then formed. Therefore, vision is the *outcome* of creative, design-based leadership rather than the starting point.

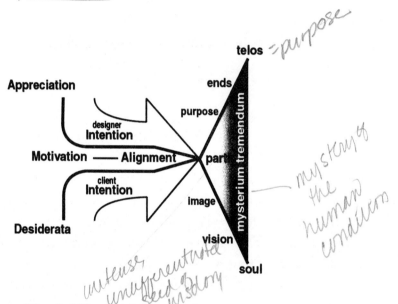

Fig. 5-4 Design Aim and Outcome

Simultaneously, this developmental process also reveals an understanding of purpose for this particular case and ultimately expands to include the general, as a representation of an unfolding telos (purpose). Just as vision is an outcome of an intentional design approach, so too emerges an ultimate understanding of purpose. Neither vision, nor telos, begins as input.

This also differs from the more traditional design process, which first develops concepts and then implementation plans. Post-

146

implementation evaluation and redesign follow production and innovation of the intended design. In all of this we notice that the parti was pre-ordained—presenting itself wide-eyed and bushy-tailed—at the very beginning of the process. Under the traditional approach, all improvement occurs during the final, redesign process, through a concrete reinterpretation of the parti. The majority of design efforts by current professional designers actually fall within this realm of redesign. The designers do not, as a rule, begin with the trigger of desiderata, but instead with a revisit to the accessible images generated from the original parti. However, if progress, rather than just improvement, is desired, the process must be initiated with the client's expression of desiderata. = PROGRESS

This is a quintessential expression of leadership in the framework of design. Leaders are required to be many things, but their most essential character is that they are designers. Leadership is not defined by a particular role, or a blend of character traits, or a position in a hierarchy, but as *the consequence of participation in an authentic engagement with the process of evoking vision from an initial expression of desiderata.*

At this point, we should note that desiderata are not the only initiating points triggering the design process. They need to be matched by an *appreciative* judgment of what is to be considered as real, in any particular situation. Let us explain what we mean by appreciative judgment. It is not a comprehensive description or explanation of what is real (Vickers, 1995). Instead, it is a judgment of what is to be treated as the essential background, or foreground, of the design situation.

As an example, when a decision is made to draw a boundary around what or who is to be included in any particular project, it is done by making an appreciative judgment. It is appreciating what is

147

important to consider and what isn't. It is an appreciation for whose interests need to be taken into account and whose do not. It is appreciating what level of complexity must be maintained as a substitute for never-ending comprehensiveness. It is within this context, and against this environment, that the design process unfolds. An appreciative judgment creates the frame for design inquiry and action, as well as the container—thus providing the limits that are so necessary in any creative work (May, 1975).

Motivation is also key to any design leadership process. In design, motivation must be intrinsic, but can be augmented by extrinsic influences as well. We'll more fully discuss intrinsic motivations in a moment, but let's take a quick look at some extrinsic motivators. For designers and others, they include such traditional rewards as money, acclaim and influence. Business literature abounds with methods for motivating people to be creative and innovative, including both negative and positive feedback reinforcements. These extrinsic forms of motivation, however, do not seem to be of critical and lasting influence.

That is clearly not the case with intrinsic motivations, which spring from a vital source, the client's desiderata. For the designer, motivation flowers from an empathy with a client's desiderata. But there are other motivations as well. Often designers speak of their responding to a call that cannot be ignored, as if they are compelled by a necessity born into them to engage in designing (Hillman, 1992). There is also the pull of what appears to be both a psychological and biochemical reward for engaging in a creative act that results in a breakthrough insight. This process of coming to emergent knowledge, through a design means, is both biologically and spiritually reinforced.

148

Beneath these intrinsic motivators resides a compelling quest for wholeness, as defined in the traditions of the *perennial philosophy*—the "immemorial and universal belief in a divine Reality" (Huxley, 1944). Designers and clients seem to understand that by engaging in design, they are expressing a god-like capacity to engage in the co-creation of the experienced world, and in doing so, make clear what it means to be human. They are expressing a deeply embedded script, which plays out the human potential to become more than we are in the present. This is the myth of Hephaistos, being played out everyday, in every corner of the world.

As Figure 5-4 indicates, alignment can be seen as a synthesis of both group process and team dynamics. Group process is necessary, but insufficient in support of collaborative design work. Group process is a bit like maintaining the operating systems of an airplane. It is absolutely necessary that all motors and control systems are kept in prime condition. This state of being well maintained and well tuned, however, does not get the plane off the ground, into the air, and onward to its destination. Flight requires the airplane to be animated by a flight team composed of flight plans, pilots, service personnel and a clear purpose for the flight. This alignment of function and intention is necessary for the design process as well. The condition of alignment integrates the intentional behavior of all the individual participants.

This is quite a task, given that design teams (as purposeful social systems) are made up of distinctly different human beings, each with his or her own unique understandings and desires. An example is the designer-client team that is inclusive of everyone with a stake in any particular design process and outcome. In effect, they are a multi-minded system (Gharajedaghi, 1999). The ability to create an

149

alignment of these independently powerful and capable minds brings focus to, and magnifies the potential within, the design process.

There are many ways in which a successful alignment can be described. A popular metaphor for this alignment is jazz improvisation. Each musician plays impromptu, yet contributes to the musical unity of a collective effort. Other musical metaphors, as well as metaphors based on team sports, point to the same felt experience of unity in diversity.

Participation in alignment has been characterized as the experience of *flow* that is an experiential state of cognition without the normal distinctions and distractions of measured time and space—an analog state of being. This concept also has application to individualized activity, as an unselfconscious experience of empathy, timelessness and unity (Csikszentmihali, 1990).

The capacities that become important to the designer, when desiderata are the focus and starting point of design, are those abilities that allow a designer to compose, imagine and make good professional judgments. Engaging with desiderata of *that-which-is-not-yet* demands creativity and innovation. It requires attention, imagination and communication in order to manifest a world not yet seen. This is true no matter the size of the design project; even the smallest design is part of that process.

Desiderata, as the initiator of design action and designed change, are the intentional links between human capacity and human achievement. They are the enabling sources of guidance for intentional human evolvement. Design is the change of evolution into an intentionally directed process rather than a consequence of necessity, luck or accident. *Reactive triggers* to change, such as fear, hate, hurt, humiliation, anger, distress and need, drain energy and hope from

150

human potential. Desiderata create energy, and hope, fueling the generative capacity of humans individually and collectively. Desiderata reflect the innate human understanding that the world is not complete as it is. Desiderata make design possible and necessary.

* that which is desired is the driver
* vision is the outcome

6. Interpretation a Measurement

Every design situation is unique and complex, constituting an *ultimate particular*, which is unique and singular in and of itself, without commensurable qualities. To create and introduce new designs into the real world, designers must know the world that already exists, in a manner that makes meaningful design possible.

In our modern society, we have at our disposal a large number of approaches to inquiry that have been developed solely for the purpose of creating such understandings. For some, the only way to reach a true understanding of reality is through the strict procedures of science. Others believe that there are intuitive approaches based on trusting our innermost feelings and bodily sensations. Still others believe that the real can only be reached through the help of a higher power, making reality accessible only through spiritual experiences. Each of these approaches offers us a way to *interpret* the world.

Interpretation is a subjective process where the real in the world is explored thoroughly, in order to understand its basic constitution. The real does not always present itself to us in a form that is necessarily meaningful or easily understood. We are quickly overwhelmed by information about the immensity of the real, as well as by its complexity. Information comes to us through direct sensory experiences, or as information we have gathered and collected from a variety of secondary sources. The challenge is to make sense out of all the information received.

Surveys, scoping, statistical analysis and direct measurement help us to discover more about reality. These approaches make reality accessible through measurement and categorization. Typically, the idea is to consider only variables that are unproblematic. So, we focus on life situations that present reality in forms that we can easily interpret, which makes it possible to understand and control them. More sophisticated approaches, with the capacity to see with greater clarity into the richness of reality, include qualitative methods, such as ethnography and context analysis. This type of investigation does not use straightforward scales of measurement, but relies on qualitative interpretations of more complex information sources.

All of these approaches are common tools in the scientific tradition. But even with the most objective, truth-focused approach, there is still a need for interpretation, and this can present a problem. Within the realm of science, for instance, we find different lines of reasoning for how to go about interpreting data. Some researchers argue that we must use methods that reveal the true core of reality, without being colored by our innate subjectiveness; while others argue that any true understanding of reality can only be achieved by relying on our own subjective ability to adequately interpret reality. Our desire is to break down this polarity. We are interested in putting forward a holistic approach to understanding the real world in design situations. To do this, we must further investigate the act of interpretation.

Interpretation, as a part of the design process, serves the same purpose as evidence and proof do in science. Interpretation is part of our attempt to grasp the conditions and context that *exist* and will set the stage for our ideas and new designs. We need to know and understand the situation we are going to change. Design, though, is not just about creating something new. It is about creating a whole, by adding something new to something already in existence. Every design must fit between the existing and the *not-yet-existing*. It is a composition. In a holistic design approach, everything is also embedded in a *context*. For designers, context consists of those things that have been selected to stay unchanged in the face of designed change. This is in contrast to *environment*, which constitutes those external things that must be taken into account, but which cannot be changed by design. Designers have to be able to observe, describe and understand the context and environment of the design situation.

There are many ways of approaching the world in order to discern the preconditions for a design. Most of these approaches have quite narrow purposes. This means they can only focus on a few limited aspects or properties of reality. In attempting to interpret the full complexity and richness of reality, we are wise to use a variety of these restricted methods. For example, if the design task is focused on creating a new organizational structure, it is common to begin by trying to define the present structure in both formal and informal terms. We might choose to conduct interviews and surveys with employees, to see how they would describe what is good and what is bad about the existing structure. We might study competitors, the marketplace, financial trends, technological developments, etc. There is no end to the breadth and depth of research that we can choose to be occupied with. There is no limit to how much data, information and knowledge we can generate.

No matter how restrictive, these traditional scientific approaches are essential to the process of understanding a design situation. The tradition of science has always been aimed at finding truth—the understanding of how things really are. Given this, science has developed tools and methods with the purpose of studying our *existing* reality and then describing it, as carefully and accurately as possible. In design, these methods and tools are invaluable as they help us to form a basic, factual understanding of the world.

But there is a difference between how *facts serve truth* and how *interpretation serves meaning*. As designers, we are not primarily interested in facts serving truth; instead, we are more interested in creating the real. Since a designer is not obligated to create something that is merely true, it is not necessary for him or her to use only methods sanctioned for the discovery of truth. Rather, a designer can use whatever approach provides the best possible understanding of reality from a design perspective. This does not mean that anything goes, or that one method of interpretation is as valid as any other method. It simply implies that the notions of validation and acceptance have different qualities in design than they do in science.

Design is intentional; therefore, design interpretations are also intentional. It is intention that predisposes us towards certain data and values. This means that interpretation cannot be done without an understanding of a direction—without desiderata. Another way of saying this is, that interpretation is an action that allows us to observe and understand the world through the lens of our design desiderata. It is a means to discover if the world holds a valence for our designs and if there is good fit between our chosen design and a specific situation.

In design, interpretation is not about determining a solution by closely and objectively analyzing reality. It is not a search for the right, true and precise design, hidden somewhere in the richness of reality. Instead, interpretation is an act of judgment. A scientific assessment is an accounting of objective factors, while a design interpretation is an appreciative judgment—a picking and choosing of what is to be considered and in what way. For example, it is a judgment that determines what will be considered as foreground and what as

156

background, what is important and what is unimportant, what is valuable and what is of little value. Whenever a part or aspect of reality is considered important enough to be analyzed, a judgment has been made. In design, interpreting reality can not be done without imposing judgment, which is guided by intention.

This does not mean that an understanding of reality based on scientific methods is useless or misguided. Rather, we would like to bring science and judgment together in a way that is guided by intention and is holistic in its approach. But this is a difficult task, since it requires a move towards meaning. Thus, it is not an approach focused on deductive or inductive scientific reasoning, but on meaning making. The making of meaning is not an activity embraced by science; however, as a designer, it is vital to your process. You participate in the creation of a real world. To do that, you need the world to make sense to you. To design is not to create things that make the world more fundamentally true, rather to *create a world that has more meaning*.

Aristotle saw attempts to make meaning out of the world's complexity as a dilemma. Nussbaum shows us how Aristotle argued that we have to accept a third type of choice and action, other than the *quantitative approach* and the *guess* (Nussbaum, 1990). For Aristotle, the third way is based on *qualitative* judgment.

Nussbaum argues that there is no reason we should be defensive about the scientific community's steadfast assertion that *measuring* is the only way to proceed if we want to be rational. For Aristotle, it was not possible to reach a true understanding of the complexity of a situation by means of science only. It is this *practical wisdom* that sensitizes us towards important aspects of a concrete situation. It is an overall judgment, where we accept the contributions of each

157

approach, without the requirement of an overall logical coherence. Aristotle argues against the idea that all aspects of a situation are comparable as equivalents. He makes a defense for *specific* judgment, prior to the *universal*, along with a defense for feeling and fantasy—as important aspects of a true rational judgment or choice (Nussbaum, 1990).

Aristotle's philosophical musings mesh well with our belief that a complex design situation needs to be approached as a whole. We can measure and analyze a situation, but any overall understanding can only be reached through a design interpretation, that is, in turn, achieved by means of qualitative judgment. As designers, we create meaning in a situation as a whole, including the systemic or emergent qualities that arise from the interactive relationships of the elements composing that whole.

When we enter into *design interpretation,* we distinguish between different acts of interpretation with different purposes and outcomes (see Fig. 6.1).

purpose	outcome
explorative interpretation	finding meaning
generative interpretation	creating possibilities of meaning
compositional interpretation	meaning of outcome emergent meaning created meaning

Fig. 6-1 Design Interpretation and Meaning

As we've said before, in any design situation, it is important to find out as much as possible about existing conditions. But the amount of information that can be gleaned from a situation is, in fact, infinite.

We can never know all there is to know and can go on gathering facts forever. As designers, we must face this reality and not expect to be completely comprehensive; instead, we must endeavor to *construct meaning* out of the complexity and chaos that constitutes the real world. This is an act of *exploration of possibility*. Because the capacity for information gathering is infinite, exploring empowers the designer to depend, not just on acquired skills, but on luck and chance as well as on intention. The availability of an infinite amount of information means a fully rational analysis of all information is not possible. Therefore, to explore any real-world situation, we are required to stay focused on purpose and desiderata, while remaining open to the possibilities that reveal themselves in fortuitous ways, since meaning is never out there to be 'found'—external to the inquirer.

A different type of interpretative process occurs when the intention is to *create possibilities of meaning*. To conduct *generative interpretations* is to imagine possible meanings. It is a way to interpret the present, in relation to the *not-yet-existing*. Reality, interpreted this way, makes it possible to visualize an infinite number of new realities. This process is creative, generative and always done in relation to the meaning produced in the explorative interpretation. The purpose of generative interpretation is to experiment with different interpretations of reality, in order to create possible futures that are in line with our intentions and desiderata. This is an imaginative process disciplined by intention and desire, while being grounded in real-world considerations. Divergent thinking and brainstorming are just a couple of examples of common ways in which designers generate possibilities.

As we introduce a third form of interpretation, it is useful at this juncture to examine the nature of interpretation from a different

159

angle. Instead of thinking of interpretation as a way to find the difference between *that-which-is* and *that-which-is-envisioned*, it is often productive to think about interpretation in relation to a *context* and *environment*. In every design situation, there are things that are impossible to change (environment) and/or things that we do not want to change (context). The context forms a contrasting background to that situation's desiderata. This is not the same thing as finding the difference between two states of reality. Rather, we see desiderata as something that contrasts with context. Therefore, we begin to compose a whole out of what already is in existence (the background) and what we desire to make come into existence. It is in this sense that design interpretation becomes compositional.

The *meaning* of the outcome of the design process is then examined through the lens of a *compositional interpretation*. Building on the other two modes of interpretation, the designer goes through a compositional process as described in the chapter *Composition*. The *found meaning* and the *possibilities of meaning* are fused into an interpretation that embodies both a holistic and systemic character (see chapters *Systems* and *The Whole*).

Design interpretation is a way to find out where we are and if we can move in the desired direction, in alignment with our intentions. To do this, we need a background or a foundation, against which our interpretations are considered. This foundation is not common knowledge or truth—instead it is the *measurements of life*. Now, what do we mean by this? We mean that when we consider the worth of our lives, we know that we are not simply measuring a set of variables.

Life is too rich and complex to be reduced to the sum of such measurements. Instead of using a set of stiff computational scales, we embrace a more appropriate technique, using the measurements of life. These measurements consist of the following: *standard of life*, *way of life*, *quality of life* and *spirit of life*. The first three can be easily contrasted and compared as seen in the examples below (see Fig. 6-2).

The fourth—*spirit of life*—is not easily put into contrasting categories of similarity like the other measures of life. However, it carries the most influence in how such things as artistic endeavors, special places, cherished people, life experiences and personal desires are given a sense of worth in someone's life. The spirit of life is much too expansive to be covered here in any adequate way—but it cannot be easily set aside. We can only recommend an honest exploration of the many spiritual traditions that have arisen in the course of human evolution, in addition to your own introspective spiritual journey.

Of these four, only *standard of life* relies primarily on traditional scales of measurements. The other three engage in interpretive meaning and value. They can be applied only by the use of intentional judgment.

In design, there is always room for traditional measurements in the process of interpretation. But, they have limited applications and should not be considered to be adequate in any design situation.

For example, in designing development policy in Indonesia, a nation that embraces hundreds of language groups and cultures, the *standard of life* measurement of calorie requirements for the average adult may be constant across the nation. However, the sources of those calories are a measurement of *way of life*, so that fish, or corn, or rice may be the preferred source for a staple food. The *quality of life* measures the taste and freshness of the food supply. The measure of *spirit of life* relates to the relationship of food to spiritual beliefs and practices. Taken together these four measurements provide one whole metric of Indonesian life. When only one or two measures are used,

161

the result is a pale and simplistic shadow of the full potential of a design approach to life.

AREA OF FOCUS	STANDARDS OF LIFE	WAYS OF LIFE	QUALITIES OF LIFE
	commensurable measurement	*nominal measurement*	*incommensurable measurement*
Environment	• Level of environmental degradation. • Cost of Preservation.	• Type of environment. • Prioritization of environmental problems.	• Pleasure from environment.
Health	• Number of sick. • Cost of health care. • Availability of services.	• Definition of health. • Definition of illness.	• Sense of well-being. • Control over healing & renewing.
Housing	• Housing quantity. • Housing price.	• Spatial allocation. • Style of construction.	• Fit betwen users' character and choice of housing & location.
Nutrition	• Quantity of food. • Level of nutrition.	• Kinds of food. • Methods of preparation.	• Sensual enjoyment of food.
Education	• Access. • Literacy rate. • Test scores.	• Curriculum content. • Pedagogy.	• Intellectual development.

Fig. 6-2 Examples of Measures of Life

162

Interpretation and measurement are at the core of design activity. They make us realize that all our creative, intentional designs have to fit into an already existing world. They also enable us to appreciate how each new design, each addition, each change, actually changes the whole. Every designer is part of the 'big' design—and every design contributes to that whole.

7. IMAGINATION AND COMMUNICATION

D esign is about bringing things into the world. It is about creating the *not-yet-existing*. One of the great design mysteries is where this *not-yet-existing* image comes from. In earlier chapters, we presented the concepts of desiderata and intention. We explored how our desires form the platform for our intentions. Now, we find that there are processes that have to be in place for this to happen. As we discussed earlier, description and explanation do not prescribe what actions ought to be taken in any design situation. They cannot determine what solutions are best for a particular design situation, or what creative insight should be implemented. The most careful scientist, using accurate instruments calibrated to the closest tolerances, cannot observe or quantify that which proceeds from the human imagination as an outcome of intentionality and purpose (*telos*). The reasoning and logic behind an accurate explanation of the existing are not the same as the logic and reasoning used to determine what is desired that does not yet exist. Therefore, principles of observation cannot transcend their own context and become an epistemological link to other frames of reference. Designs of inquiry always have their own unique rational structure and internal logic.

One of the processes most people think of when design is mentioned is creativity—to design is to create. But bringing something into the world involves much more than pure creativity. It is a long process with two major ingredients: *imagination* and *communication*.

In order to create, one must have the ability to *imagine*. Imagination is demanded in all fields of design, no matter what the situational demands on the designer are. Even a very restricted design situation, one that is similar to many previous cases the designer has encountered, requires a certain amount of imagination to create the composition for that specific situation. This means that every *ultimate particular* design must be created by imaginative thinking. It can never be fully imitated or copied. Every situation must be imagined anew.

Imagination is also inherent in the process of interpretation. To imagine what parts, variables and aspects of reality are important in a specific design situation is a truly necessary skill. Architecture, organizational design, curriculum design, urban planning, information systems design, industrial design and social systems design all demand designers able to conceptualize and give form to their ideas in a way that makes them communicable and comprehensible to everybody involved in the design process.

The ability to give form to an idea can be described (using a concept borrowed from Kant) as the *formative faculty* of the designer (Makkreel, 1990). In his thinking on the formative faculty, Kant had been strongly influenced by his contemporary colleagues, but he broadened the original scope of the concept to include a whole range of *imaginative skills*. Kant showed the importance of recognizing formative skills focused on at least two different categories of objects: *given* objects and *non-given* objects.

In design, there is a need for formative skills in both these categories. Unfortunately, they are not always regarded as equally important. Often, the formative skill required for the design of given objects is accorded far more emphasis. These are the skills required to make a good representation, or *image*, of something already existing. This overemphasis on the given, versus the non-given, leads to a situation in which most designers are not sufficiently skilled in the art of making non-given objects (new design ideas) visible, communicable and understandable. The formative faculty for non-given objects has to be recognized as an important skill in all design fields (Stolterman, 1999).

The nature of formative powers, or imagination, has always been part of the philosophical debate, even if it has seldom been acknowledged as a major question for philosophers. The act of imagining has not been emphasized in traditional disciplines. This is predictable, when you consider that science has, as its major purpose, the creation of new knowledge about reality—the given. There has not been the same kind of interest concerning how to change reality through the process of imagining and inventing new realities.

Kant also mentioned other modes of formative faculties that range from direct, sense-based formations, to completely imaginative formations. They could be said to reflect their relative degree of dependence on the material world. For Kant, the imaginative formation "does not have its cause in real representation but arises from an activity of the soul" (Makkreel, 1990).

Kant also made another distinction between formative powers based on temporal relations. He talked about *direct image* formation (in the present), *reproductive image* formation (about the past) and *anticipatory image* formation (in the future) (Makkreel, 1990). Using these distinctions, it becomes clear that design is an act of anticipatory image formation. It is an act where we have to imagine the future, the *not-yet-existing*.

To Kant, it was also obvious that all three modes of formation are dependent on *imagination*. Imagination is needed not only when we want to make up the future, but also when we are called on to describe the past or present. A situation can never be described exactly as it is.

167

Every description of the past or present is based on a choice of the attributes of a situation that are important enough to bring forward in time or hold in time using the faculty of imagination. This kind of decision can only be made using well-developed imaginative skills. Based on this, we can conclude that no matter what kind of formative actions we are engaged in, imagination is always at the core of that activity. Also, we need to note that there is no such thing as a straight-forward depiction of something—a 'direct image' formation—without the involvement of imagination and judgment.

Imagination slowly emerges as the foundation of all types of formative activities. It is also a basic skill underlying other design fundamentals, such as interpretation, composition and judgment. The ability to imagine is required in virtually every step of the design process.

A designer relies on his or her formative skill to transform ideas and visions into something that's possible to share with other people—this means he or she must render non-given objects into images of what will become given objects. Imagination is therefore something different from creativity. Creativity is the spark that ignites the emergence of novel ideas that have the potential to become normal ideas. These ideas are seminal, integrative and cohesive. They are formed from latent, autonomous elements of experience and intuition—forged from within an individual's life experience.

Creativity is often described as the creation of new and viable ideas, with the implication that this means creating new truths—as in science. Graduate students at universities are regularly required to engage in literature searches to assure that their own creative research leads to a new truth, which can then be added cumulatively to the body of information containing every other seasoned truth. New

168

truths can be the product of creative thought in this way, but this is not the limiting criterion for creative thinking.

Creative ideas are often situational and particular rather than universal. In other words, creativity is the process of bringing forth that which is new and novel in the life of the inquirer. A creative thought, act or product is creative if it is new and novel to the creative thinker, within the context of their lives. It is not required to be unique among all thoughts, acts and things, anytime and anywhere, although it might be. It is also not required to be true always and everywhere to be considered a product of creative thought. It is only required to be a new and novel product of an individual's imagination in the real world of that creative individual, with the potential to become a viable part of that world.

Imagination gives form to the creative idea as an image. It is, in effect, a type of skill than can be practiced and trained. But, being able to imagine how a new design might look, feel, act and behave in a given situation is only one side of the coin. A designer must also be able to communicate that image.

One of the most common and persistent beliefs among the general public is that designing is primarily drawing and drawings are designs. Patterns of decoration are defined as design—as are plans and schematics. Many dictionary definitions reinforce this perception because the list of possible meanings of the term design begins with these basic understandings. Visual representations are important elements in design communication, but they are far from being sufficient. Among the list of dictionary definitions there are usually one or two that refer to design as a *form of intention*. It is this definition that is most closely related to the meaning of design which is explored in this book.

169

The communication of intention involves more than the creation of visual representations of finished design ideas. Design communication is essential throughout the whole design process and is heavily dependent on the creation and communion of images. Images are fundamental to human communication whether with others or ourselves. We all have experience with the phantasmagoric flow of images in our dreams that Sigmund Freud considered communication between the *id* and *ego*. Many of us are also aware of the universal images, or archetypal images as Carl Jung called them, which all humans seem to share in common. Images are primal and a rich means for human understanding that go beyond text and speech. Although words may evoke images, they are not a substitute for them.

Therefore, design communication is not merely text or language dependent—design communication is image based as well. For example, the popular creative technique of 'brainstorming' is a group verbalization process used extensively by product designers, organizational consultants, community activists and others working with teams of people. The verbalization approach has limited effectiveness when used in isolation, because true creativity is image rich as well as image dependent. However, when a collaborative, language dominant technique is used as part of an inclusive design process—to assist in the generation and communication of images—it has much greater potential as a truly creative tool.

Design images are diverse in appearance and substance. They can be found anywhere along a continuum from complete and total psychic abstraction to literal representation. In the idealized design process, images are created deep within the psyche of the individual, transmuted and communicated to the mind's eye. This newly formed image is further transmuted and displayed in the realm of sense data.

This process is reversed or repeated many times within the confines of an individual's mind. This is as true for the client's images of desiderata as for the designer's breakthrough creative insights. This internal communication process is eventually linked to others: design team members, decision-makers, stakeholders, producers and others involved in the design process. This external process is most often a developmental process involving communicating images that are being translated into less abstract, more concrete versions of themselves, with iterative feedback loops along the way.

Design communication between designers and clients is somewhat unique in that this involves a process striving to re-recreate the internal image development process—in reverse—in the 'other'. A translation of an external sense data image into an internal image in the mind's eye is then translated into an image in and of the psyche. When the 'other' is the designer, the outcome is empathy. When the 'other' is the client, the outcome is service. Engaging in design communication at this level is to engage in a design conspiracy—a form of systemic intimacy that is synergistic of, but not suffocating to, individual gifts of imagination.

There are any number of ways to communicate design images. In this chapter, we make the case for a particular method of design communication that fits the intention and character of design and serves the variety of people involved in the process, including both clients and designers. It honors the complexity of thought processes that are dependent on both solitude and collaboration and also enhances individual strengths and group synergy. It is a process that allows a design team to expect the unexpected outcome, in alignment with the client's desiderata.

171

This is an *allopoietic design communication process*, different in kind or degree from other types of communication in both form and purpose. Design is a process of making something on behalf of the *other*, similar but not identical in meaning to the German term *kunst* (creating something outside of self). Therefore, a design communication system must be one that can support *poiesis* (a Greek term for the process of making something) with the expectation that it is not merely making as an instrumental process. It is the act of creating something intentionally on behalf of another's desires and purpose—it is design. A related process of making, one that can be characterized as being on autopilot, is called *autopoiesis* or self-making. *Allopoiesis*, on the other hand, is a term meaning *other making*. The making of something outside of one's self, with and on behalf of the other (see *Systems* chapter).

This type of inquiry involves imagining and creating *that-which-does-not-yet-exist*, but which we desire to be in existence, in the service of humanity in general and specific people in particular. It is about the significance of human intention and purpose in the creation of the real world. (This is in opposition to the typical Western approach, which prescribes that something *ought* to be done, simply because it *can* be done. This assumed link is typically lifted from a frame of reference of an economy where money—as the measure of value and economic return on investment—stands in for any deeper aspirations.) Humans have an immense capacity to cause things to come into existence, for good or ill, which nevertheless becomes the reality of our experienced world.

The ability to communicate or consummate images of *that-which-is-not-yet* is essential in this process of imagination. Communicating the non-given is different from the process used to communicate

172

inductive or deductive reasoning; communication that is used in the realm of description and explanation. Communicating *that-which-is-not-yet* is a nonlinear, dynamic process that grows out of the systemic relationships among individuals engaged in the design process. Each individual plays a different role and brings different skills, perspectives and authority to the intentional process of taking actions. In turn, this causes new forms to come into existence where none existed before.

These relationships encourage the communication of desire, purpose and imagination. They include the communication of images, which are, by necessity, diverse and unique in nature. This includes the communication of individual perspectives of trust and common intent, of common and uncommon understanding, and information necessary for collective action.

In order to facilitate the use of imagination to create rich images in the service of human intention and in support of design judgment, we need a special type of communication, one that works both intra-personally and interpersonally. For successful design communication, the use of prose, spoken or written, is necessary—but not sufficient. Visual communication, utilizing approaches like cognitive art, graphic design and virtual reality modeling, is equally important, but still insufficient. All of our senses contribute to the work of the imagination—creating images—but the imagination labors in the realm of non-sense as well. Therefore, design communication is dependent on both sense and non-sense as carriers of the design messages. It is a form of communication that is both phenomenal and noumenal. It is dependent on sense data, and at the same time, inde-pendent of it. Reason and logic inform it, yet it is equally independent of the laws governing formal logic and reason.

Communication modalities, such as formal *dialogue* or *visual literacy*, are essential to the process of making design images concrete realities. Yet, as powerful as these methods are, they are not sufficient when it comes to successfully conveying the emergent images and insights of a design imagination.

Formal dialogue (the Greek term *dia-logos* refers to creating meaning through words) is very effective as a collaborative communication method (Isaacs, 1999). It is a process for gaining common understanding and common meaning among individuals in a group. This method is quite useful whenever members of a design team or group need to reach a common understanding of the past, present, or a future situation. But these dialogues are not designed to reach into imagination's depths and extract new ideas.

Visual literacy and cognitive art utilize denotative signs and connotive symbols, graphics, schematics, sketches and other types of concrete images to convey complex ideas by taking advantage of the eye's extensive cognitive capacity (Tufte, 1983, 1990). In addition, music and other non-visual types of communication appeal to other natural senses, helping to form shared understandings in diverse and divergent ways. But, shared understanding is just a part of the requisite communication needs of design.

Design communication needs to convey comprehension, meaning and the promised value of *that-which-is-not-yet*. This can be done through the utilization of *diathenic graphologue*, which means to let a thing be seen through its image. One way of understanding the complexity and richness of *diathenic graphologue*—the communication of the non-given—is within the context of that which we have called an *allopoietic* design communication process (see Fig. 7-1).

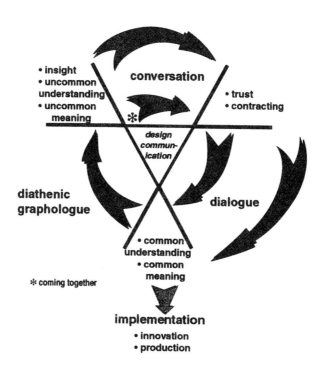

Fig. 7-1 Design Communication

This design communication process unfolds through four iterative stages and one implementation stage. The first one, *introduction*, is followed by iterations of the next three, *conversation, dialogue* and *diathenic graphologue*. After an adequate conceptual design has been developed and agreed upon, we enter the last phase, which is the implementation phase of *making*. In the case of design, implementation takes form as *innovation*—the transformation of the creative concept into a concrete particular addition to real life. Of

175

course, in reality, projects are probably not this clearly delineated by step and phase. Yet, the process remains true in spirit to the ideas behind allopoietic design communication.

Although the arrow of time flows through these stages in sequence, the sequence is not necessarily linear—it is sequentially emergent. This means that the subsequent stages are dependent on the outcomes of the preceding stages. The initial step reflects the obvious need for initiation of contact with the 'other', the potential design clients. The contact can be a face-to-face connection, or it can be an empathic connection with clients who can never be in a face-to-face situation (e.g., future generations), or who cannot represent their own interests to the fullest extent (e.g., children). It can, to a lesser extent, be a customer whose needs are represented by governmental or corporate providers acting as surrogate clients.

The first phase of design communication begins with the triggering of the design imagination within each individual designer. The explicitly and implicitly communicated needs and desires of the clients initiate this response. The ability to convey and listen to the other is at its best when the exchange is heard as if it's a *conspiracy* (i.e., a breathing together) of *conversation* (i.e., a turning together). To have a conversation is to explore the other; to find relations and connections that can serve as starting points for contracts and fuller relationships. This is a very sensitive process, in which the possibilities for emerging contracts and relationships must be carefully developed. The ability to go slow, to be patient, from a first contact to a full conversation, are the building blocks to a good designer/client relationship.

The conversation phase is followed by the second phase, known as *dialogue*. With dialogue, there is a move towards a shared under-standing and expression, motivated by the desire and intention of the

176

specific situation. This phase of the process is essentially the creation of a common understanding among those within the process. It is not a process of identifying a truth that has been carried in from the outside by an expert participant. It is not a give-and-take process of coming to compromise, where pieces and parts are either accepted or rejected, as part of the common ground. It is simply reaching a common understanding, given the particular context of people, time, place and resources. A dialogue can be designed in many different ways. It is important that the way the dialogue is set up is in resonance with the people involved and the specifics of the situation. To reach a common understanding does not mean that everybody has to have the same understanding of the situation—it only means that everybody is clear about one another's understanding.

Once common understanding is reached, it is time to move towards *uncommon understanding*. The *not-yet-existing* cannot come from an understanding of the present only—it has to come from the imagination of the possible as well. This third phase focuses on *diathenic graphologue*. The process transports newly-formed seminal images of *that-which-is-desired* from the birthplace of their creation, from within a single individual's imagination, connecting them with feelings and emotions along the way, where they're imprinted with details from the color and texture of the histories of the clients and the character of the designers. They make their way into the shared conscious world of the senses—to be more fully formed and synthesized in collaboration with other designers' formative imaginations (see *Composition* chapter for a more fully developed description of this process). These seminal images trigger new, emergent or divergent images in other's imaginations that can become triggers for even more

177

images. At some point, a judgment is made that an image is sufficiently rich and mature for the next stage of this phase.

These matured images are then encoded with communicative artifacts. Diathenic graphologue affiliated approaches, such as cognitive art, are intended to evoke the experiences legislated by the images. This allows clients and others to feel, imagine, or be moved by the sublime quality of the ordering principles of these images—images that embody the clients' expressed and unexpressed expectations. They allow critiques by designers, clients and other stakeholders to be expressed fully and authentically.

Acceptance often comes in the form of surprise at recognition of met expectations, embodied by images that have emerged from the creative imagination of an individual designer further refined and transformed by others. Neither client nor designer could have imagined these images on their own, or held these images *a priori* to the design experience. These candidate images arise from an individual intimately bound to others in the systemic relationship of service. The uncommon idea becomes the common ground for intentional change. This occurs when the creative insight of an individual is transformed into a commonly shared experience among designers, clients, decision-makers, stakeholders, surrogate clients and essential others.

Design communication becomes cyclic at this point, moving from the process of gaining uncommon understanding, to transforming this into a common understanding and then back again into an uncommon understanding and back yet again…you get the picture. This cyclic process can occur as many times as there is time and need and until the adequate has been reached. At a point when an adequate common understanding is wrought from uncommon images, the process transitions into one of making the commonly imagined a concrete part of the real world. The artifact then takes on its own life history, contributing both intended and unintended outcomes to the lives within its sphere of influence.

A designer's formative powers are needed both in the process of coming up with the unexpected idea and in giving form to that idea so that it can be communicated. Imagination and creativity are so closely related in design that one is almost worth nothing without the other. Yet, creativity and imagination, alone, are not of any value without the ability to communicate. Good designs must be given form and communicated.

In summary, imagination is not only needed as a way to create the unexpected, but also in the process of interpreting the present—the client's needs and desires, as well as future demands and possibilities. Imagination is the reflective skill we use to explore and analyze the overwhelming number of ideas that are possible in every design situation. By imagination, we can visualize future compositions and explore the consequences of bringing a particular into existence.

179

8. JUDGMENT

Judgment is a key dimension in the process of design. The ability to make solid *design judgments* is often what distinguishes a stellar designer from a mediocre one. Now, how are we defining judgment? By judgment, we mean that which is at the heart of wisdom, in all of its manifestations. For us, judgment is the means and wisdom is the outcome. In fact, wisdom can be defined as good judgment, which enables right action and appropriate change.

Judgment is a form of decision-making that is not dependent on rules of logic found within rational systems of inquiry. Judgment is not founded on strict rules of reasoning. It is more likely to be dependent on the accumulation of the experienced consequences of choices made in complex situations. Judgment is not irrational, because it follows its own dialectic. Learning to make judgments is not a matter of learning to follow the steps of a technique, or to follow directions dictated by a method or algorithm, or to impose the *a priori* constraints of a theory.

> What one acquires here is not a technique; one learns correct judgments. There are also rules, but they do not form a system, and only experienced people can apply them right. Unlike calculating-rules.

> L. Wittgenstein (1968)

Judgment is, by definition, an elusive animal. It is as distinct from rational decision-making as it is from intuition. Judgment has practical, pragmatic value and academic legitimacy, without having to be codified and generalized, as science demands on behalf of its cousin, reason. We believe the capacity to judge can be learned and then applied in design circumstances, without destroying its essence and value. This is unlike the case of intuition, where too much intellectual attention is often feared by artists who feel that reason, at its best, is the opposite of intuition, at its worst, a mortal enemy. The ability to make good judgments is as essential in design as it is in business, law, medicine, politics, art, or any other profession. For a skill that is necessary to so many endeavors, it is surprising that judgment is so little understood and so seldom a part of one's formal education. There have been some significant exceptions to the lack of attention that is paid to the formal development of the concept of judgment.

For example, Immanuel Kant, the German philosopher living in the eighteenth century, placed judgment as one of three cognitive faculties of human beings. For Kant, meaningful propositions were not just the consequence of empirical fact or analytic logic. They were also the consequence of *normative* judgment. In addition to his categories of judgments of fact, he developed philosophic concepts of judgments of ethics and aesthetics as well. His concept of *aesthetic* judgments (Kant, 1790) does not focus on the same outcomes as the concept of design judgments developed here, but there is some influence nevertheless.

John Dewey (Dewey, 1910) stated that there is an intimate connection between judgment and inference. The intention of inference is to terminate in an *adequate* judgment (which is equally a *good* judgment) through the interpretation of facts. According to Joseph Dunne (1993), John Henry Newman, a nineteenth century Christian apologist, proposed that judgment was made possible by the intervention of the *Illative Sense*, which informed reasoning leading to

182

correct judgment. In Dunne's book, he develops his own, well-grounded, argumentation for judgment, by elucidating the distinction between the two Aristotelian forms of knowledge, *techne* (a Greek term for productive, technical knowledge) and *phronesis* (a Greek term for practical, personal knowledge). From this, Dunne argues for an understanding of 'practical wisdom' that makes it possible to take the complexity of reality into account.

Contemporary examples of judgment-focused scholarship include the seminal contributions of C. West Churchman (1961). Churchman defines judgment as a 'well substantiated' belief, a belief held collectively by a group, in contrast to a belief held by an individual. As mentioned earlier in the *Desiderata* chapter, Sir Geoffery Vickers (1995) is known for his development of the concept of *appreciative* judgment in public policy design. Appreciative judgment is the capacity to understand, or *appreciate*, a situation through the discernment of what is to be considered as background and what is to be considered as foreground, in the formulation of a project context. Horst Rittel, another example of someone who has formally developed a concept of judgment making, focused his attention on the fields of design and planning (Rittel, 1974). Rittel went so far as to state that every logical chain of thought is ended only by an *off-hand judgment* (one of several types of judgment he considered) and not by reasoned decision-making. Most recently, focus has been put on decision-making in high stake situations that are ill defined and time constrained—a form of judgment referred to as *naturalistic decision making* (Zsambok & Klein, 1997).

A lack of appreciation for judgment as a legitimate means of decision-making is not only revealed by its absence in curriculums and professional discourse, but by the negative connotations one hears in everyday conversations regarding judgment. These conversations are full of comments that are indicative of the distrust of judgment: "Don't judge me." "Don't be judgmental." "That's only your judgment."

Judgment can best be understood when it's considered within the context of knowledge, knowing and the knower. To put it simply, judgment is *knowing* based on *knowledge that is inseparable from the knower*. By this, we mean that judgment is based on accessing knowledge that is generated in the particularity or uniqueness of a situation; knowledge that is inseparable from the knower and is only revealed through the actions of the knower. This is in contrast to decisions that are made, based on knowledge that is of value primarily because it is separable from the knower.

Judgment knowledge cannot be stored in libraries or on databases. Colleagues in controlled experiments can't replicate it. Neither can it be memorized nor accumulated in any quantity so as to build a field of expertise. Judgment knowledge has instrumental value only for a particular situation and loses its direct and immediate relevance in the next setting. Therefore, it becomes clear that separable knowledge deals in that which is universal, or generalizable—while the inseparable knowing of judgment deals with particulars and ultimate particulars. This implies that designers can learn to make better judgments, but cannot learn—*a priori*—the kind of knowledge necessary for particular judgments at the moment they occur. Skills and competencies can be practiced and mastered, in support of future actions, but should not be confused as knowledge for judgment itself. Scientific knowledge, the ultimate separable knowledge, plays a necessary supporting role in good judgment making, but it is very different in character from the knowing that's embedded in judgment.

184

Knowledge that is separable from the knower is an end point in a continuum that transitions from data, to information, to knowledge. There is no similar continuum in relationship to judgment-produced knowledge. There is, however, a direct connection to wisdom. Sagacious action has been considered as evidence of wisdom and the source of such action is always good judgment.

We will use these general definitions to examine judgment—particularly design judgment. We argue that a better understanding of the concept of design judgment and its different specific manifestations is needed, if we want to intentionally improve our design ability. Although design judgment cannot be separated from the designer, the designer can reflect upon the nature of judgment making and begin to approach the ability to make good judgments as an essential key to gaining access to design wisdom.

Unfortunately, judgment is often framed as an inappropriate means of decision-making. It is also deemed to be an inappropriate foundation for action or belief. Judgment is put into the same category as mere opinion or conviction, which, since the time of Socrates, has not been considered a legitimate form of knowledge in the Western tradition. Thus, it is not considered to be a fit candidate for accessing design wisdom, the necessary precondition for right action. It is paradoxical that when others want some demonstration of our personal accountability we often receive the advice to "trust your own judgment."

Judgment is also touted as the enemy of creativity. Students of creativity are constantly admonished to suppress their judgment, to hold it in abeyance and allow the free flow of their ideas to emerge. Creativity and innovation are often proffered as the polar opposites of judgment. In reality, though, well-managed judgment is a necessary component in the synthesis of creativity and innovation. Without exercising judgment, creativity is diffuse and innovation rootless.

Where judgment is acceptable is in day-to-day settings in the arenas of life that traditionally require judgment calls to be made. Judges are required in sports and beauty competitions, in order to decide who is the most beautiful, or to make decisions on what is fair play, what is worth a game penalty, or whether a specific behavior is good sportsmanship or not. Judgment takes on its most serious role in the realm of law. In this case, judges are expected to make considered judgments based on their own experience, as well as their understanding of the qualitative and quantitative truth of a particular situation, in relationship to an idealized code of law.

And, lest we forget, there is another form of judgment that has concerned humanity for millennia, often called 'the final judgment'. In this situation, a Supreme Being sits in judgment of an individual's life, in anticipation of the inevitable end of worldly existence and the beginning of eternity. The anxiety and fear of this form of final judgment filters into attitudes about more corporeal forms of judgment that carry the threat of punishment from some authority figure. Police, judges, bosses, parents, teachers and others with positional authority are surprised by the negative reaction against their potential for authoritative judgments. The antagonistic reaction to this kind of ultimate authority and power, over the measure of an individual's worth, results in the rejection of the idea of judgment altogether.

Our distrustful attitude toward judgment is quite fascinating when you stop to consider that people are engaging in judgment all the time. It is as common as breathing. In fact, nothing would ever get done, without the small judgments being made by people all the time.

186

This is because real life is complex, dynamic and uncertain. Truth is difficult enough to know even with the best science, but reality, the domain of human experience, can be overwhelming and beyond comprehension. Careful, accurate description, concomitant with clear explanation, is necessary but not sufficient in the quest for enough understanding to allow wise decisions to be made.

Therefore, without the capacity to authentically use judgment, there often emerges a situation, commonly cited as 'analysis paralysis', and its frequent companion, 'value paralysis'. These two types of paralysis result from the popular assumption that decisions need to be based on a comprehensive understanding of the specific situation. Further, this comprehensive understanding, imbued with rational logic, will eventually lead to the 'correct' solution. It is also assumed that this approach renders results not influenced by any personal preferences. In other words, that it is an objective and unbiased process. Due to their ambition to be comprehensive, approaches like this often lead to oversimplifications.

This is because to be comprehensive means to deal successfully with an unimaginable amount of data and information. In order to deal realistically with the complexity and complication of large amounts of information, within a reasonable amount of time, it is necessary to find ways to simplify. This means ignoring or leaving things out that cannot easily be characterized. It also means using generalized abstractions to stand in for the multiplicity of particular constellations of sense data. In the process of simplification and generalization, nuances and subtleties are lost. Even things that are obviously apparent are lost because they are not easily understood and conveniently accessible through descriptive or explanative frames of reference. There is a danger in not dealing with the full richness and complexity of reality.

The value of judgment is that it allows individuals to overcome their paralysis and engage in the messy complexities of life in a way that, when done well, can bring function, beauty and meaning to human existence.

Formal, rational, decision-making processes are often held up as the standards to be used by businesses, governments, institutions, foundations and individuals, when one must engage in complex, dynamic issues. The irony in this is that decision-making, based on rational analysis alone, actually creates more options and divergence than it does convergence (in the form of focused outcomes). This is true, even when there are resources and time enough to allow a comprehensive process to unfold. On the other hand, judgment relies on a convergent process. It brings diversity and divergence into focus; that is, it brings form and meaning to messy real-world situations. Best of all, it is 'on time' or 'in time' which means that it takes place within the constraints of a reasonable time frame based on a time line of realistic expectations and limitations. This is the discipline of judgment. It is making good judgments in a timely way without the delays associated with never-ending studies.

We believe that judgment is a basic human activity. But, what exactly is this phenomenon? Is there just one kind of judgment? No. Reality presents itself to us with a full richness that has forced us to develop different forms of judgment to match the diversity. In any complex situation—where there is a particular purpose and need to make decisions and take actions—we rely on a number of types of judgments. These include: *intellectual* judgment, *practical* judgment,

188

ethical judgment, *systems* judgment, *professional* judgment and *design* judgment.

These various kinds of judgment relate to specific aspects of our experience of reality. People use these judgments to deal with the problems, questions and challenges they face. Keep in mind that we never find any of these judgment types in their pure form; there is always overlap between them. Because we are interested in how judgment affects us as designers, we will take this opportunity to focus more intently on the phenomenon of *design* judgment.

Design judgment holds many things in common with the other categories of judgment, but the outcome is distinct because it deals with volition and desiderata. Design volition—using one's own will to pursue desired ends—forms the distinct character of design judgment. Design judgment facilitates the ability to create *that-which-is-not-yet*. It is a form of judgment related to creative and innovative processes and is concerned with the *compositional whole of the imagined design*. When design judgment is executed well, it can create beauty and evoke the sublime.

Design judgment is essentially a non-metric decision or understanding. That is, it does not rely on a science of measurement to determine an objective or subjective outcome in its deliberation. Design judgment is the ability to gain insight, through experience and reflection, and project this insight onto situations that are complex, indeterminate, indefinable and paradoxical. This results in the emergence of meaning and value, through the creation of relationships that cause the appearance of unity, form, pattern and composition, out of apparent chaos. Judgment is, in effect, a process of taking in the whole, in order to formulate a new whole. The outcome of judgment is not predictable based on rational anticipation. Nevertheless, the outcome of good judgment complies with the criteria and constraints supporting the driving intention and expectations of any particular decision-making process. The operational outcome of any judgment is dependent on the nature of the intention. Intellectual judgment may lead to an understanding of a general principle, while design judgment leads to a concrete particular understanding, within a contextual setting.

In our examination of design judgment, we have found that it actually encompasses several different types of judgment. For instance, as designers we face situations where we have to make an overall judgment on the quality of a specific material used in a design. At other moments, we have to judge how the chosen parts of a design fit together as a whole—as a composition. These two situations are not only different in their focus, they also reveal how different the act of making a judgment can be, and how our skills and knowledge underlying a judgment may differ.

We do not claim that the types of judgment presented below are the only possible ones and we want to be careful to recognize that we are only talking about *design* judgment—this is not a discursive, generalized theory of judgment. Also, this not an attempt to define design judgment as residing in the realm of the *true*; instead this is a concept that dwells in the realm of the *real*. It is an attempt to create an image of design judgment that is practical enough to help designers and non-designers better understand how designing works and improve their capabilities and skills as designers.

Reflecting on design judgment, we can initially distinguish between *client* judgments and *designer* judgments. We can also divide design judgment into a *conscious* or *unconscious* act. In Figure 8-1, this is visualized as being inside or outside the circle, where the inside symbolizes

190

unconscious judgments and the outside of the circle represents conscious ones.

Before we explore designer judgments, let us briefly discuss client judgments—judgments that are made at the conscious or unconscious level, or at the boundary between the two (see Fig. 8-1).

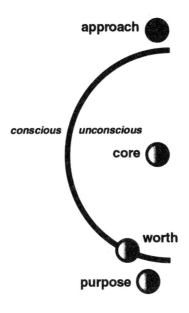

Fig. 8-1 Client Judgments

A client, first of all, has to make the judgment of intention. For a client, it is always possible to choose—or not to choose—design as a way to *approach* a situation. The client can make the judgment that design is not the appropriate approach and may instead choose problem solving, a scientific approach, or even a management or spiritual approach. *Design is, in every situation, only one of many options.*

191

And, sometimes design is not necessarily the right option. If a client needs a process that will lead to a guaranteed and predictable result, design is not appropriate. This is because design is the act of creating the *not-yet-existing*, which, by definition, is always a risky business. This judgment of approach, if made in favor of design, marks the entry into a design project and is always made by the client.

Once within the design process, the client must make a *judgment of purpose*. It is the client who has to make the overall judgment about the purpose of engaging in a design process. This does not mean that the client necessarily will decide what has to be the outcome of the design. By this judgment, the client will set the stage for the design process and also provide the designer, or design team, with a first approximate direction for all energy, thoughts and actions.

In the design process, the client is also responsible for making judgments of *worth* or *value*. A designer can never make that judgment on behalf of a client. He or she might be able to suggest, or try to influence, or educate a client to appreciate certain qualities and certain design consequences, but the final judgment of the worth and value of a design is in the hands of the client.

These client judgments ought to affect the designers' judgment on whether or not to serve the client in the first place. The making of these seminal judgments by the client not only creates restrictions on possible actions by the designer, but also instills accountability and responsibility by the designer, concerning the systemic effects of the judgments. Because of the mutual influence clients and designers have on one another, there is rarely a clear demarcation between these client and designer judgments. This means that the judgments of the designer have an impact on the clients' realm of judgment. These initial judgments are also modified and refined throughout the design process by the cross-catalytic effect of judgments being made in the different domains of responsibility.

It should be obvious, at this juncture, that the client does not merely provide an entry point into the design process. The client plays an ongoing role throughout the design process, by having the responsibility for the judgments described above. Design judgments are never made once and for all. New ideas, creative changes, changed preconditions, and increased understanding and knowledge all change the context for the judgments made. Judgment in design is fully dynamic and dialectic, between conscious and unconscious judgments and between client and designer judgments.

Designers are expected to make a lot of judgments and are held accountable for their consequences. These judgments are not all of the same type; going well beyond the difference between being conscious, subconscious or a negotiation between the two (see Fig. 8-2). Depending on which category of judgment the designer is engaged in, different strategies and tactics are demanded, which require different commitments of time and energy.

The entry point—or gateway—for a designer into a design process is marked by an altruistic judgment of whom to serve—the judgment of *service*. Once this judgment is in place, with all its concomitant relationship-building, contracting and related activities, a design project can be initiated. Within a project, we divide designer judgments into ten different types. These judgment types can be described in detail, but here we will only briefly introduce them. Our purpose is to make the case that a better understanding of design judgments is fundamental to the further development of a designer's skill. Just as the client is responsible and accountable for client judgments (approach, purpose and worth), the designer is fully responsible and accountable for the ten presented here.

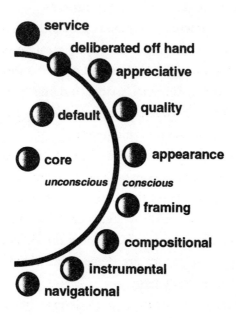

Fig. 8-2 Designer Judgments

Default judgments are *off-hand* judgments, made without deliberation, as an almost automatic response to a triggering situation. In some ways, default judgments resemble instincts, in how decisions are made and actions taken. The difference is that default judgments can be introduced where they did not previously exist; they can also be modified and refined, or replaced by new ones entirely, whereas instincts are genetically based and unalterable. These judgments are

194

expressed as a 'bodily knowing', enabled through kinesthetic intelligence. In the craft tradition, they are an *artless art*—an apparently effortless application of high-level skill without conscious deliberation. Action is taken without recipe, formulas, or deliberation. A designer often encounters situations where default judgment is used. It is usually seen as a sign of experience, when a designer can make good default judgments in pressing situations.

Default judgments are accessible through the process of *deliberated off-hand* judgments. A good example of this concept is learning how to ride a bicycle. As many of us remember, this begins with full attention and deliberation, until our judgments of balance become second nature and no longer require conscious attention. Riding a bicycle then becomes a known skill that we have acquired. Learning to drive on the left-hand side of the road (after initially learning to drive on the right) is an example of the process of surfacing off-hand judgments—to bring them up from their habitation in the unconscious and modify them by making them open to deliberation. Every unconscious move must be surfaced, consciously inspected and modified. This often happens in an environment of extreme complexity, with overwhelming sense data barraging the driver. After some period of time, driving decisions can once again recede into the unconscious realm of off-hand judgment calls. All skills are developed in this way, whether they are in sports, arts, or manual labor.

Appreciative judgment, as developed by Vickers (1995), is a matter of appreciating any particular situation from a type of gestalt perspective. By this, we mean determining what is to be considered as background and what needs to be paid attention to as foreground. It is a process of assigning importance to some things, while not to others, without the intervention of hierarchy. This form of judgment is key in

195

the determination, or appreciation, of what is to be considered as context in a design situation.

An *appearance* judgment is complex and multi-layered. It includes determinations of style, nature and character. Stylistic considerations are made by determining if a particular judgment outcome is something that is preferred. This can be made because the choice is enjoyed as a personal preference and looks attractive, or feels preferable due to a sense of familiarity, comfort, or membership in a larger context of similar actions, or things. This type of informed judgment is not guided by a literal matching of attributes on a one-to-one basis, as is the case with scientific correspondence, which is used to create rational taxonomies—groupings based on logical similarities. Instead, an appearance judgment is grounded in the kind of certainty that comes from a strong sense of self-assurance, stemming from membership in a group, which values certain qualities by consensus.

Judgments about appearance—as related to the *nature* of that which is being designed—are concerned with the material substance of the design. This is quite different from judgments that are made about the *character* of that which is being designed. Considerations about character concern qualities such as form, essence and excellence. Character is about the appearance of difference, as a consequence of being unique, singular, or even odd (Hillman, 1999).

Appearance and *quality* judgments often seem related, but there is a significant difference between them. Appearance is usually associated with taste. In taste, there is a presumption that desired attributes are recognizable in an identified collection of concrete particular examples. In this case, the challenge of judgment is to determine whether there is enough similarity between the proposed and the existing. Most designers know what is 'in style' in their specific field of

196

design. But styles do change over time, sometimes fast and dramatically. It can take a lot of work to stay in touch with what is 'in'.

However, *Quality* judgments do not have this external template to look at. These judgments are made within the confines of the concept itself, without reference to similar examples. Concepts like craftsmanship or artistry point to an understanding of the unique, in contrast to those things that are mass-produced. The quest for excellence in the creation of things of beauty, sublimity and practicality is often considered when a designer makes decisions regarding quality. Quality judgment also relates to the complex relationship between the designer's personal preferences, the desiderata of the client and the richness of the situation.

Instrumental judgments are the basis for the *artless art* that highly skilled craftspeople speak about, when referring to their interaction with their materials and the tools of their trade. This sensibility is what Jim Platts refers to as *competence* (Platts, 1997). Instrumental judgment deals with the choice and mediation of means within the context of prescribed ends. It is the process of *mediation* that considers not only technique and which instruments to use, but proportion and gauge, as well. This is the form of judgment that takes technology into consideration. Just as justice and mercy must be mediated in the crafting of a just society, any type of crafting requires a form of instrumental judgment that melds absolutes into the realm of possibility. Mediation is not a process of averaging or compromise. Mediation is a process of instrumental intervention between absolutes or ideals. Mediation between the chisel, the unbreakable, and the stone, the easily broken, results in the appearance of the desired sculptural form. Mediation is about the retention of difference in processes of unification through composition. For example, a design team is a formation of diverse

197

individuals that does not compromise their integrity as unique human beings. Mediation is at the heart of the application of skill and talent, through technology, onto inchoate material with the intention of attaining a desired end.

The ability to make the right choices in an environment that is complex and unpredictable is the ability to make *navigational* judgments. The outcome of this type of judgment is based on securing the desired state for any moment, in the moment. At a basic level, this is survival. At another level, it is the ability to gain advantage in the moment. At the highest level, it is making choices that will contribute to a larger social good. These choices are not predetermined and are, therefore, only accessible in the moment. This type of judgment is essential in many aspects of human life.

Navigational judgment does not mean "doing it by the book." It is the ability to formulate essential situational knowledge that is applicable to the conditions of the moment. It is ability gained by the experience of utilizing this competency and the experience of the consequences of doing so. Navigating ships is an archetypal form of this type of judgment.

> The experienced navigator will sense when to follow the rule book and when to leave it aside. The 'right rule' in such matters is simply: do it the way an experienced navigator would do it. There is no safe guarantee at all, no formula, and no shortcut. And yet this absence of formula does not mean that we have laissez-faire, or that any choice one makes is all right. There are many ways of wrecking a ship in a storm, and very few ways of sailing it well.
>
> M. Nussbaum (1990)

For instance, navigational judgment is important to managers and, as a consequence, this skill is taught in schools of management through the methodology of case studies. These studies provide the student with virtual experiences of navigational judgments, made in concrete, particular business settings. In the same, way novels and storytelling provide larger, more complex examples of navigational judgment that have relevance beyond institutional boundaries.

Framing judgment is a key form of judgment in the design palette. This judgment is at the very heart of the deliberation which determines the adequate. It is used for defining and embracing the space of potential design outcomes. It is also used for forming the limits that define the conceptual container—a *virtual* crucible—that is required for containment of the intense *heat* of creative activity. Finally, it is used for determining what is to be included within the design process, and what lies beyond consideration. Framing judgment can elicit the most anxiety because it is the most divergent from a designer's belief in the comprehensive, or holism. Holism, or complete understanding, has great intuitive appeal, but is not as important to design judgment as may be imagined, especially from an absolutist perspective.

Framing and containing is what is needed in the early phase of design, when the designer faces the full complexity of a real design situation. Hit by all the demands of the client, with a feeling of having too little resources or time, with a conviction there is not enough information readily available—anxiety can creep in. Still, as a designer, you have to be able to act. You have to start the design process by setting the stage, by framing the situation. This means you will find yourself intentionally deciding to ignore some aspects, in order to focus on others. In the same way that a photographer chooses what will be included in his or her photo and what will be left out, the designer must make framing judgments. To an inexperienced designer, this may be the most difficult judgment to make. Before it is made, all possibilities are still open, while afterwards, the design process is limited. It is a judgment of great importance. Often, after a designer has become experienced, he or she finds this is one of the most rewarding stages in the design process.

The signature judgment type among the different manifestations of design judgment is *compositional* judgment. This type of judgment is at the center of the creative process and includes aesthetic, ethical and rational considerations. Using compositional judgment, relationships are created among a palette of elements, with an eye towards calling forth a compositional whole. This whole displays the qualities and attributes particular to the unique character of the ultimate particular, thus serving the design intention most adequately. This compositional whole is formed with the aid of the guiding domains of aesthetics, ethics and reason, but not in the mode used in analysis. The difference cannot be understated. Unlike the famous example of blind men describing an elephant while touching different parts of the animal, the function of compositional judgment is not to create a synthesis of different perspectives but to create a composition out of difference. The point is that there is no 'elephant' *a priori*, just waiting to be described and explained—there is nothing yet. Compositional judgment is seminal to the creation of *that-which-is-not-yet-in-existence*.

Core judgments are buried deep within each individual, but, unlike off-hand judgments, they are not so easy to access. Core judgments make themselves known when one is being pushed by why questions. At some point, the process of deliberation stops, because it is at this point where meaning and value are fixed. By *fixed*, we do not mean in the sense of the biology of instinct, but fixed in the sense that creating, modifying, or rejecting these core judgments takes a great deal of effort in both time and intensity. We all know the uneasy feeling when we are challenged at a level that we recognize as 'who I am'. We lose our ability to argue in a rational way. We might even react like children, when we cannot justify our side of the argument, but still feel deeply that we know what is right. See Collingwood (1939) for a discussion of the nature and influence of 'absolute presuppositions'.

Even if core judgments are buried deep inside us, they seem to be accessible through at least four channels: character or 'genius', life experience, creative experience and experience of the sublime (see Fig. 8-3).

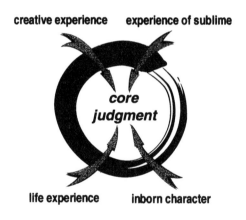

Fig. 8-3 Dimensions of Core Judgment

Inborn character is the concrete particular identity which comes into the world with us, as a promise waiting for fulfillment (Hillman, 1996). Core judgments seem to respond to choices that either contribute to this fulfillment, or detract from it. Also, core judgments are a composite of meanings and values, formed during the *experience of living*. These are not the products of reflection, or deliberation, but are embodied as lived experience. As life is experienced anew, the influences of old experiences are modified and new meaning and values are infused into one's core. In addition, the experience of the *creative* process, which results in a deep insight of consequence (i.e., not just a matter of cleverness or cunning), contributes to the creation of new meaning and value. This new understanding becomes a part of the designer's datum for core judgments. Finally, an *experience of the sublime*—an experience that moves us and transcends senses, feelings and emotions—can also cause movement at the core. There may be other ways to influence a person's core, but these four seem to be access points to core judgment, which we can attend to most carefully.

So, in summary, both clients and designers are elements in a compound relationship, which is animated by the interaction of many different types of judgment. Judgments are continually being made, and then refined, throughout any particular design process. Each set of judgments, whether designer or client related, must be made by the accountable individual(s) within the appropriate role. If, for instance, clients allow the designers to make judgments of purpose and/or worth, then the process becomes one of art, rather than design. If, on the other hand, the clients are encouraged to make judgments regarding composition, or framing and containing, then it becomes a process of facilitation, rather than design (see *Service* chapter).

The key idea is that design is a system of relationships, which include a variety of roles and responsibilities (such as designers and clients), from which design activity, and outcomes, emerge. It is a composition that depends on the interaction of different design roles

202

for the emergent quality to be produced, in the same way that flour, sugar, eggs and other ingredients combine to form the attribute of flavor in the material we call cake batter. Cake flavor is an emergent quality, not present in any of the ingredients when tasted in isolation. Similarly, the role of designer is not the defining element of design. For designerly activity to be expressed as an emergent quality, designers, clients and all other design roles must be in the mix.

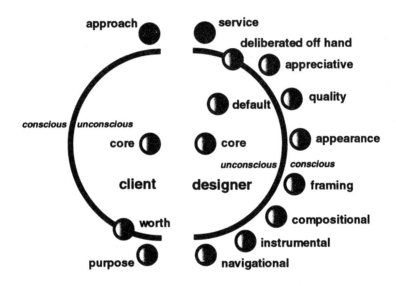

Fig. 8-4 Relationships of Judgment

Figure 8-4 shows a plethora of judgment types. It creates a rich picture of complex relationships. In a design situation, neither the client nor the designer can use this 'map' as a guideline. Its purpose is simply to make us realize that design is a process, fully guided by design judgments of astounding variety and type. There is no temporal aspect in the map and there is no priority to the type of judgments necessary. In real situations, these judgments are made all the time in a complete dialectical relationship. Of course, certain design processes do demand more of specific kinds of judgment, while others demand less. Yet, the map is still valuable as a tool for reflection and for an intentional attempt to improve one's design ability. The map can even be used as an analytical tool. Such an analysis might be helpful, to explore one's own way of approaching a design task.

We need to add one more type of judgment and that is *mediative* judgment. All the presented judgments will, in one way or another, contribute to the final design. A designer needs to make judgments on how this whole should be judged. Thus, he or she must balance and proportion, the different types of designer judgments, through *mediative* judgment.

The *designed whole* is the result of all the judgments made in a design process (see Fig. 8-5). It is a synthesis of three holistic domains: the adequate whole, the essential whole and the significant whole (these ideas are further developed in the *Composition* and *The Whole* chapters).

The meaning of the whole, in relation to judgment and design, is one of the most crucial aspects of design, in effect, distinguishing it from other traditions. Design judgment has a special character, since the resulting design is something produced by imagination, something *not-yet-existing*. In its various forms, design judgment relies on all our capabilities as humans. It is based on intellectual and conceptual thinking, as well as aesthetic and ethical considerations and its fundamental starting block is the character of the designer.

As stated at the beginning of this chapter, we believe that design judgment is a full and equal partner in intellectual pursuit, on a par with rational decision-making. Design judgments are not jeopardized by an improved understanding of their nature; as opposed to the mystery of intuition, which can be threatened by too much self-consciousness. The judgments that constitute design, as illustrated in this chapter, are based on the conviction that it is possible, through intentional intellectual effort, to understand and improve our capacity and skill in making any judgments—particularly design judgments.

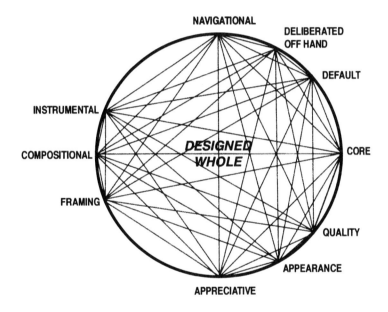

Fig. 8-5 Design Judgments

Again, we should emphasize that we are not talking about making *true* judgments. Instead, we are talking about treating design as an aesthetic and purposive form, whereby we make the imagined real, using our ability to make good *adequate* judgments. Design is about making critical judgments, ranging from reflexive off-hand judgments, to judgments emerging from our core being. It is about an appreciation for the whole and all its systemic relationships. Therefore, being more reflective, in order to understand more about the activity of judgment, will not interfere with a designer's ability to make good design judgments. It will only help to improve those judgments.

This way of understanding design judgment leaves us, as designers, fully responsible for our judgments and our actions. There is no way to escape from this responsibility. Designers, in relationship with the client, have complete responsibility and accountability for their designs. This is because they have chosen, based on their design judgments, to make a particular conceptual design a concrete reality, without the protective cover of the truth. This leads us to the conclusion that good design is possible to achieve. The process of achieving it can be improved by learning to treat design as an informed process of intention and not something gained simply by chance or necessity.

9. COMPOSITION

A design is always a composition. To design is to be creative and innovative, but more importantly, design is to cause things and/or people to stand together as a unified whole—a composition. Creating such a system of unification means bringing parts, pieces, functions, structures, processes and forms together in such a way that they have a *presence* and make an *appearance*, particularly of unity, in the world. Composing is an integration of several strategies of unification. These strategies use rules of relationships (protocols), in the creation of compounds, functional assemblies, patterns, systems and wholes.

Visiting a museum, where art objects are placed in a large room, is an aesthetic experience. It is an experience in two ways. The first is fairly obvious, as each art object creates an aesthetic experience in its viewing. But there is also the experience of viewing the exhibition itself as a design—as a composition. We are attracted to each individual object by the way it is related to, and under the influence of, the wholeness of the exhibit. In a similar way, a new car consists of many parts, each with its individual purpose, structure and form. They all contribute to the design of the car in different ways. When we approach a new car, we might have different tastes reflected in preferences for individual elements, but we are affected and influenced by the composition of the car as a whole.

Individual elements in a composition are made to acknowledge each other, to fit a certain style or intention. Maybe they are similar in the way they are shaped, their color or texture, or in the way that they behave. Sometimes they are made to contrast, or create tensions, as part of the overall design strategy. For example, in organizational

207

design, this would be achieved by introducing creative change agents into a highly structured company with strong intrinsic stabilizing forces. Sometimes the elements of a composed whole may integrate into a coherent blend. Sometimes they may stand in stark contrast to one another. In either case, they are always part of the *composition*.

Every intentionally formed design is given comprehensibility and meaning through its specific composition. That composition is the intrinsic *ordering system* of the ultimate design. A composition is not just patterns of parts, but a whole that displays emergent qualities, which transcend the qualities of the elements in isolation, or summation. In addition, the *substance* of this composition gives a design its sense of integrity. This substance is reflected in a variety of ways including the composition's character and appearance.

The act of composing is pragmatic and inclusive. To compose is to realize and accept possibilities and restrictions governing the design challenge. This does not mean that a designer's work should be dictated to by real or imagined restrictions. Neither should he or she be constrained to predetermined possibilities. Restrictions, as well as *a priori* conclusions, must always be carefully examined and challenged. This is true even of the needs and constraints presented to the designers by clients and other stakeholders in the initial contracting phase of the design process.

Composing is based on a thorough understanding of what can be done, what should be done, but most of all, what is desired to be done. A composition should emerge in response to what has been found to be the client's most authentic desiderata. At the same time, composing is also pragmatic, in the sense that it is an act of finding an *adequate* solution. It is making judgments as well as reasoned decisions. To compose is to engage in design judgment on an ongoing basis.

208

It is not the intent of design to search for the *absolute* solution, or the one *true* answer, to a design challenge. Designers must compose a whole that adequately responds to the intentions of the client, in relation to a particular context. Composition is an act of creating the *particular* or *the ultimate particular*. There are no universal, *a priori*, compositions for generalized design applications. There is only the specific in design composition. As such, there is little gain in copying or imitating earlier designs. There is no need to survey other designs, with any other purpose than to stimulate creativity and catch a sense of the mood of designing as an activity, unless it serves the purpose of historical or critical interests.

Even though there are no standard or universal solutions, studying earlier designs helps designers become aware of the specifics of each unique design situation, of the design judgments made in response, as well as of the final outcome. This immersion in the totality of past design projects develops a *sensibility* and *appreciation* in designers for the process of composing an ultimate particular design, but it does not provide pat answers for future designs.

Composing is an activity where judgments are made, using aesthetic principles like balance and symmetry, about relationships between details and the whole. When Rudolf Arnheim (1995) writes that the goal in design is to create "a symmetrical, coherent and well-balanced whole," he is pointing to this important aspect. It is about making judgments on how to best integrate a particular design into a specific context and about how to match a design's actual potential to the clients expressed desires.

These *framing* and *compositional* judgments are creative acts. Designs express creativity not because they may consist of new innovations, like the latest high-tech materials or novel social functions. Rather, creativity is expressed in the way things are brought together—in how they are composed. Understanding design creativity to be a form of composition, we can now see how many activities—not commonly considered as such—are acts of design.

For example, the formation of public policy, the creation of new educational programs and curriculum, the design of one's own life, the formation of intentional communities of interest, the development of entrepreneurial business plans, or the development of a new philosophy of life, are all compositional designs. Understanding the nature of composition means more than having a familiarity with the inventory of relationships of relevant elements and domains of application, it means understanding design as a process—a compositional process—as well.

The general design process has had many representations throughout time. This includes the archaic 'four stages of the alchemy process', which interestingly enough, is as representative of the creative design process as many of the contemporary models of creativity developed by psychologists and creativity consultants (see Fig. 9-1). Besides being a fascinating early metaphor for the design process, it introduces an adjunct metaphor of the essential design *crucible*, which is an intentional construct of the designer made anew for each new design situation. The process of going from *unknowing* to *insight* (from lead to gold) requires the presence of an effective crucible—one that can hold the 'pressure' and 'heat' of such a dynamic process, mentally or materially, by defining the sure limits, and therefore the space, within which the process is enabled to effectively unfold. Without such a container, it is impossible for the process to take place. This is especially true, in more pragmatic terms, of real-world design. Limits and space need to be defined through the presence of a design culture, a design environment (studio culture) and the particulars of a design project as defined by client's desiderata.

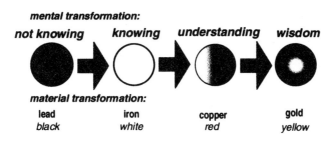

Fig. 9-1 The Alchemy Process

In addition, the monomythic Hero's Quest, synthesized by Joseph Campbell (Campbell, 1968), is another representation of the general design process (see Fig. 9-2).

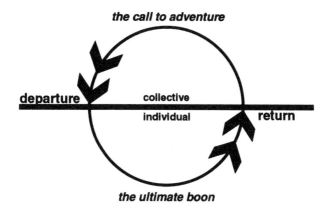

Fig. 9-2 Monomythic Hero's Quest

211

The mythic journey of separation from the collective conscious and entry into the individual unconscious ends with the questing individual's return back to the collective conscious, in possession of a boon or insight, in service of the collective's good. This hard won gift erupts into the real world, to be rejected or accepted, depending on the interrelationship between the traveler and the collective. It is a process fraught with danger, flavored by fear and anticipation, much as the medicine man is feared and revered simultaneously for the services he performs and the benefits he provides to the health and vitality of traditional communal life.

In a more contemporary version of the design process, as presented here, the sudden appearance—or *emersion*—of an idea that represents a design *solution*—a *parti*—identifies that part of the design process that is characterized as creativity. The condensation of parti, the formative germ, from the swirling clouds of imagination, occurs at the intersection of dramatically different composing activities, sub-conscious uncontrolled and conscious controlled, and is often experienced as a sudden flash of insight, a breakthrough thought that is typically referred to as the *ah-ha* experience. It is an explosive appearance of a *simulacrum*—an encoded solution to a complex design challenge—a parti (see Fig. 9-3)

Fig. 9-3 Emersion—Breakthrough Insight

This *emergence* phase in the design process is marked by the precipitation of a viscous, rather than crystalline, nucleus idea. From this formative ideal—a 'liquid' seed—a mature design concept grows. It is the initial germination of an idealized form. The parti can emerge in a singular moment, or in a drizzle of proximate moments with equivalent effect.

The phases in a design process that are of particular relevance to composition begin at the point of *emersion* and end with *innovation*. This involves a transitioning from the *particular ideal (parti)* via the *particular real*, culminating in the *ultimate particular* (see Fig. 9-4).

Fig. 9-4 Steps in Design Related to Composition

These consecutive phases of the design process consist of two very different forms of composition. The initial phase is a subconscious, uncontrolled compositional activity, resulting in the spontaneous appearance of parti. The second, or terminal phase, is a conscious, controlled compositional activity (see Fig. 9-5) resulting in a fully matured design concept ready for innovation.

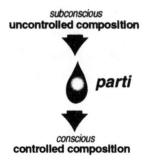

Fig. 9-5 Parti at Intersection between Two Types of Composition

A parti is a compelling organizing template, guiding the designer in the succeeding design process steps. The parti is the seed of an ideal compositional form. It is similar to the *logos spermaticos*—the seed idea—of the rhetorician's persuasive argument. In the case of design composition, the parti is the *grafos spermaticos*—the seed image of an ideal composition—to be used to form a real, particular design solution.

The parti is essential, enabling a designer to draw together, to compose, a complex set of elements into an integral whole. It is this binding ideal, which the designer, in a leadership role, is then obliged to turn into something real—with accessible *presence* in the world.

214

A compelling parti helps the designer to make many types of judgments and decisions in order to create a whole. To be sure, a parti, or *guiding image*, is fluid, always "tentative, generic and vague" (Arnheim, 1995). But, for the designer, this vagueness is not a drawback. Instead, it opens up a whole range of possibilities, without commitment to any one of them. Arnheim writes: "Being undefined in its specifics it admits distortions and deviations. Its pregnancy is what the designer requires in the search for a final shape."

The design process is typically misrepresented as a 'problem solving process' and a design challenge is miscast as a 'problem statement'. Designing does have a problem solving phase. However, it is quite different from the case where 'problem solving' is treated as the dominant strategic intent of design.

The parti, as the conceptual whole of an ideal design solution, is impossible to apprehend or communicate fully, without being transformed into images, or schemes that become accessible as real, concrete particulars. Therefore, a design 'problem' is the perceived difference between the elusive ideal solution, as represented in the parti, and the realistic, pragmatic schemes needed to represent it as closely as possible in concretized terms.

This would indicate that designers problem-solve using a form of *design dialogue* or *diathenic graphologue* that involves the formulation of design schemes, as *particular real* compositions. They do this through an iterative process of scheme formulation, comparison to the ideal parti, further scheme development and additional comparison to the ideal solution (see Fig. 9-6). This iterative process includes clients and other stakeholders, who become intimate with the essence of the parti through the emerging concrete images of the schemes. The test of a good parti is when clients recognize that their desires and needs have been met, or exceeded, by the emerging design being communicated through these images.

This iterative design process is continued until a judgment is made to cut off the design dialogue and focus on the development of the scheme, which has been deemed an adequate, realistic representation of the ideal solution (see Fig. 9-6). This design dialogue should never be terminated because of measurements of perfection, efficiency, or comprehensiveness. The design dialogue should be cut off because of judgments such as adequacy, essentiality and significance.

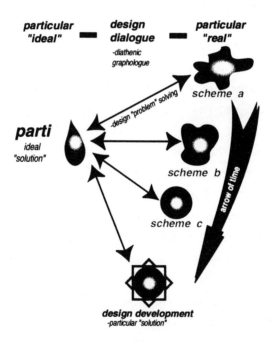

Fig. 9-6 Design Problem Solving

Although the initial composition process, leading to the emergence of the parti, is uncontrolled and takes place mostly at the subconscious level, it is possible to prepare and facilitate the process through intentionality. Because of this, there can be an expectation that the parti that emerges embodies all the attributes and qualities that were intentionally stirred into the super-saturated 'solution', which abruptly transforms itself into a solidified insight. It also assures that the parti is not a random product of novelty-generating creative behavior, focused merely on indulgence and not purpose.

As we mentioned earlier, design skills, especially skills in composition, can be developed through focused reflection and analysis of earlier designs. It is also possible to develop design skills by critiquing existing designs. Each time a designer formulates a critique, he or she further develops a sense of the particular, of the integration of details into the whole, of how the integrity of a design is manifested through its form and appearance—how all of this holds together as a composition.

Compositional skills also include the ability to *envision* and *evaluate* a design that is *not-yet-present* but only imagined. These skills require a compositional foundation based on creativity and imagination, combined with a pragmatic sense of what is real, what is controllable and what is appropriately not controllable. Learning to hone these skills requires a different means of gaining competence. Traditional educational designs just don't cut it. Design learning should be understood as learning how to fuse—to bring together or to compose. The development of critical and analytic thinking skills, a dominant focus of education, ought to be balanced with creative and synthetic thinking skills in order to facilitate the development of compositional

217

competence. In addition, a curriculum based on systems thinking, which is an essential intellectual foundation of design, supports compositional learning by providing a logical framework in support of composition.

The *terminal composition phase*, the process that is controllable and operates at the conscious level, can lead to excellent schemes or mediocre ones, depending on the design skills, tools and competencies of the designers. In either case, this final compositional form is the design that will become present in our world and will represent, for good or bad, the parti's essence. Clearly, the parti is held captive to the ability of the designers to translate its potential into reality.

This terminal composition can also be understood as the sum of fundamental *design principles*, as implemented in the concretized design. However, a composition is not the same thing as its corresponding design principles. At this stage, composition is not just about process—it is also about the actualization of such principles.

Because something is a composition does not guarantee good quality, or good design. We can find many low-quality, bad and even evil compositions in the world, including in buildings, products, urban design, organizations and institutions. We can see mediocrity in all the things where the relationships and symmetry between elements, structure, function and form are inadequate, ugly, or morally wrong. In some cases we experience this, because there is an absence of an intentional, underlying composition. This is typically the case when we find an artifact or system incomprehensible, with no emergent qualities or any sense of wholeness.

Although design compositions are consciously formed through the intentional actions of designers, other types of composition can emerge as the consequence of discrete decisions and actions not aimed

218

at the creation of compositions informed by a parti, but ones that are formed by accretion—growth and development by incremental additions. But even these accidental compositions are the consequence of agents acting, although unconsciously, as composers.

If a designer fails to transform the parti into a composition that forms a viable addition to the real world, then his or her design will not be recognized as an autonomous system, process, or artifact, with integrity and unity. In other words, the terminal composition must be a conceptualization of the parti expressed in the experienced world, as an ultimate particular design.

In our discussion, we should note that there is still another translation that needs to be made. That is from final composition to *appearance*. A composition can be given *presence* in the world—can be made to *appear* as a design in the real world—in whatever way the designer deems appropriate. There is no single correct appearance for any composition. There is any number of appropriate ways to give a composition its appearance in the world. This, too, is a matter of design judgment.

A design's ultimate appearance can hide or reveal its true nature, its character and its soul. The most immediate form of appearance has to do with its presenting features—the qualities that inform the senses most directly. The nature of a design can be both trivial and significant at the same time. Designs gain significance by carrying meaning through such meaning making elements as affordance, representation, association and information.

Style or fashion is often taken to be the essence of design, yet it often represents the most superficial level of appearance. Appearance, in addition to *style*, is also manifested through *nature, character* and *soul*. A critically acclaimed artifact of high fashion may, at a deeper level of

219

appearance, reflect a character of gluttony and the soul of indifference in a design environment requiring sustainability and commitment.

Looking at a face, your own or another's, gives you a sense of age, skin tone, shape of face and color of eyes and hair, revealing a person's style and nature. But, it is the next level of appearance that comes closer to the truth of the person. That is the appearance of character, which is revealed through a more discerning means of sensing who this person is, as a *unique* individual. Looking into the 'eyes' provides access to yet another level of appearance, that of soul, the *spiritual essence* of the individual.

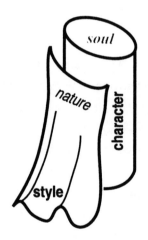

Fig. 9-7 Levels of Resolution of Appearance

Similar levels of appearance can be manifested in compositions (see Fig. 9-7). These are levels of resolution that require attention from the designer, if his or her design is to be fully realized through the emergence of appearances at every level. The appearance of a design can be treated superficially, in which case its value to people may be no more than its superficial nature. Deciding what level of appearance to attend to is, once again, a design judgment.

As stated earlier, designed artifacts are most commonly recognized by their most immediately accessible level of presence, their style or fashion. Style and fashion are characteristics of presence that appear across the compositions of the one designer, or school of design, or across eras of material culture. When particular design principles are used together regularly and consistently implemented in multiple artifacts or system designs—a style is born. Some traditional design schools have used the idea of style-specific compositions as their organizing strategy for curriculum and pedagogy. On occasion these styles have become famous, e.g., the Bauhaus style in material culture. To anyone familiar with the Bauhaus style, it is possible to recognize a design as that style without knowing the particular designer. However, some styles are reflections of certain cultures, or societies, and came to be without having been the consciously designed compositional trait of one individual. Most people can recognize Scandinavian furniture design, or Japanese home design. This recognition occurs because the characteristics of these general styles have become so well known and widely used. The same is true for organizational and social systems design such as represented by religions and cosmologies.

When a system is formed but not composed, it can still serve a function, which will most likely be that of a cause-and-effect assembly; a simple system without any unifying form, with only local or regional organizing principles—a *tectonic* design. The Internet is an example of such a design. People have a difficult time trying to create an image of the 'Web' as a whole. In similar fashion, systems like the American economy are difficult to map or comprehend, because they too are not compositions—merely accretions.

If a composition is done with grace, it will give the resulting design a satisfying sense of wholeness. If well presented, the composition gives users an overall comprehension of the design, where everything relates and each detail contributes to the whole. This helps to fulfill the design's purpose and function. The design will then have the appearance of a teleological whole—an *architectonic* design.

At this point, we should note that when one works composition-ally (architectonically), the relationship between details and the whole is always taken into consideration. This implies that every single detail is vitally important to the whole. Given this state of affairs, a designer can quickly wind up with a crisis of complexity, if his or her focus on details is not balanced with principles of organization, such as systems thinking. A systems approach allows complexity to be taken into account without leading to paralysis. Systems thinking provides skeletal design logic for dealing with this kind of complexity (see *Systems* chapter).

Once a design is complete and put out into the world, it's not always easy to decipher the underlying elements of its composition. This activity demands a certain amount of skill. Sometimes, a strong impression is made by a certain design's presence, but the reasons for this impression may be difficult to deconstruct simply by viewing the whole. A composition can be subtle and elusive, requiring a highly developed skill of discernment. Every scale of measurement, including ethics and aesthetics, should be used when evaluating compositions. Once evaluated, compositions will be judged to be efficient, effective, good, just, frightening, evil, beautiful or sublime—depending on how the client and other stakeholders (including the environment and

222

future generations) are ultimately affected—a judgment on design judgments.

The ultimate evaluation is prophesized by the designers and verified by the real world. The real value of a composition is determined by its success in meeting the desires of the client and the intentions of the designers. Its intrinsic worth is further determined by the unexpected presence the design exhibits on its own, as it becomes an agent of influence and change, thus, in effect, recreating its creators.

Composition is an almost overwhelmingly important aspect of design. To compose—to shape the world—is a great responsibility, as the designer and his or her design becomes part of the ongoing creation of our reality. That can seem a daunting prospect, but once the designer dives in fully, it is one of the most inspiring and rewarding activities imaginable.

10. PRODUCTION AND CARE TAKING

Design is often dominated by creativity, its most glamorous trait. While the creativity it takes to imagine new ideas is clearly important, it's easy to forget that there are other, more down-to-earth aspects of design that are just as influential. A new idea is not worth much if it is not made manifest in the world. All designs must be innovated—i.e., made real. They must be crafted as concretized products. These other, less star-studded design activities—which deal with bringing design concepts into the real world—we have chosen to call *production*.

Production is not a process defined by force, but rather, by *care taking*. Wise production allows for the nurturing and maturation of a design. All designs need a *care taker*, someone who lets it mature in security, thus allowing it to reach its full potential. The close relationship between care taking and production means that the design can not be handed over to anyone who is not authentically involved in the design process.

Production is also not a process characterized by indifference but rather by *carefulness*. Essential attributes, such as quality, excellence and aesthetics, are gained only when close, careful attention is paid to both the process and the design itself. Carefulness is giving one's full attention to the work at hand in full measure of the design's worth.

Production should not be separated from design. When it is, the design does not mature in consonance with the formative ideas underlying the design. This chapter explores the nature of the process of bringing a design into the world. It's a delicate evolution, one in which authentic attention (notitia) must be paid to the maturation of a design, especially during times of vulnerability to external influences.

We will focus on two aspects of production; the care of the material of design—its *real* substance—and the management of the production process. Our basic assumption is that both aspects need to be founded on an understanding of carefulness—a concerned attention and care taking—a protective trust.

The fact that we can distinguish between the act of creativity and more pragmatic activities does not mean they are separate in the design process. The practical partner of creativity is *innovation*. Innovation is defined as the actual realization of something new in the world, which then becomes a part of peoples' lives. Whereas creativity is founded on imagination and inspiration, innovation stands on ingenuity and skill. Creativity demands an open mind with the ability to cross and expand conceptual boundaries, exploring new ideational terrain. In turn, innovation requires experience, a sense of limits and a feeling for material.

Innovation is by nature sequential and episodic, making it very different from creativity. When it comes to the actual production of designs, the manner and order in which things are done makes a critical difference. For instance, in order to facilitate a designed change in an existing social structure, there must first be a letting go of the old structures and materials, through a process of grieving for lost things of value and meaning. This must be followed by a remembering of the best of things as they were, to become part of the design context, and ending, finally, with a turning to the new order of things.

To be able to produce a new structure, whether abstract or concrete, social or physical, necessarily means that the material must be appropriately chosen. To produce a form presupposes instrumental knowledge of the nature of both material and structure in unity, a skill-based imperative of steps that must be followed for expected outcomes to be realized. Therefore, there is a practical order to this process—an arrow of time.

Material, as we use the word here, is not limited to physical materials like water, iron, paper and life. It also applies to the abstract material used to compose the design of a process, or a symbol, or system, such as number, essence and nature. It even applies to people as social, cultural and spiritual material. Materials are what a designer puts together in compositional relationships, creating real things. Materials are used to bring a design into existence in the world, to make it *appear* in a *real* sense.

The real world always 'speaks back' to the designer through the materials he or she has invested in the design. Donald Schön (1983) found in studies that designers frequently use the materials in the design process more or less as design partners. When the designer chooses a material and starts to use it to bring the design to life—the 'material speaks back.' It does this by showing the designer limits and restrictions, as well as opportunities, impossible to imagine without having them voiced in some real way. A simple example is what happens when we begin to put our thoughts on paper. Our own words present themselves to us in a way that reveals our thoughts. When we read what we have written, we usually want to re-write, or even re-think, our thoughts. Design material speaks to us in a way that our mind cannot anticipate by itself. In this process, carefulness is essential. How ideas are brought into the world will impact how they mature developmentally.

The way design ideas make it into the world is, therefore, a critical part of the design process. Producing good designs requires building

227

successful relationships with the material of the real world. As the world speaks back and the designer is joined in a dialogue, we move out of a polarity between the objective and the subjective into a holistic relationship. That which is innovated now becomes part of the process itself. When a design is brought into the world, there is no longer a distinction between *that-which-is* and the *not-yet-existing*. In this conjunction, we see the real nature of our designs and how they become a part of the world.

To make this holistic relationship as strong and natural as possible is one of the most challenging aspects of design. Innovation is the phase in designing where we can experiment with this relationship. Through the innovation process, a designer has the opportunity to try new ways of realizing an imagined design through prototyping, modeling, simulation, etc. Prior to innovation, the concepts of excellence or quality are just abstractions.

This points out that the production phase of innovation is not an addendum to the design process. Indeed, the design process does not disappear with the production of specifications. Designing is a process that extends through the entire time that a design is in use as part of the real world. Sometimes, the design process even extends beyond the life span of the artifact itself. The concept of 'evolving design'—design as a never-ending process—is gaining acceptance. This idea changes the basic relationships between the designer, the clients and the end users in the design process. For example, the evolving elements of a design often need to be handled separately when responsibilities in the design are contractual. Designs like computers, airplanes, educational programs and corporations are examples of designs that continue evolving through generations of particular designs.

228

The issues of excellence and quality come into focus as they make their appearance in the production phase of design. Many of the qualities that make a design complete are not created until the innovation process. There is no way to judge the overall excellence of a design before it is made real. It is only when the design is placed in its final setting that all of its qualities become apparent and visible.

In the production process, the responsibility for care taking can land in the laps of several different groups of design team members. For each group, there is a time and place where they have primary responsibility for the design. These team members include designers, clients, end users, managers and other stakeholders. The design itself will 'travel' from one subgroup of the design team, to another, at the appropriate point in the design process. For example, in the case of product design, conceptual designers may hand the design off to prototype designers, who in turn hand off to production designers. In the case of policy design, there can be a similar hand off process, only with different names for the custodians.

The production process is cared for by people with complex and contradictory demands, needs and wants. A young design's journey, from conception as a parti, to a final and full presence in the world, is both dangerous and long. To survive and develop in the anticipated way, its design process must be carefully managed. Thus, we can see the importance of design management.

If design is about bringing the new into the world, then design management is about the careful handling of that process. Design management must be based on a thoughtful understanding of the fundamentals underlying design thinking and practice. To care about the design process means one must be inclusive of all aspects of design—even if those aspects at first seem contradictory and incompatible. Design management needs to be done with the same appreciation for design that guides the creative design phase.

In the production process, there is always a tension between the need for being surprised by the outcome and the need to know with some certainty that the outcome will be on time and of the quality expected. The client and the designer want the design process to produce the *expected unexpected*, since that is the reason they have chosen a design approach in the first place. At the same time, they do not want to be surprised by something unacceptable. The process must be handled in a way that fosters both creativity and control. It is a process of managing tension.

Since creativity leads to the unexpected, the process must be flexible in all aspects. The design process has to be open to changes triggered by new insights and ideas, or in response to the 'world speaking back', even by changing contextual conditions. At the same time, our need for control demands some stability. If stability is not present, there will be too many variables changing, too much information, too much richness and uncertainty. Stability makes it possible to reach some degree of certainty. Yet, stability and control, without creativity, pave the way for only an expected outcome. When absolutely everything is under control, there is nothing to surprise us.

It is not uncommon to portray these inescapable tensions as the result of opposing forces that beg to be resolved (see Fig. 10-1). It is not a matter of becoming more consistent or efficient. Design actually thrives on these tensions. Designers have to take care that the wholeness of the process is managed so as to accommodate these unresolvable, tensional relationships.

230

attribute	process	
	creative	controlled
purpose	destabilize	stabilize
behavior	open	closed
outcome	unexpected	expected

Fig. 10-1 Examples of Tensions in the Design Process

Tensions are best understood as symmetrical relationships. It is a relation in which one cannot exist without the other. The process of design, especially design management, is characterized by these dialectic, symmetric tension relationships. Design is always practiced in the midst of contradictory needs, demands, restrictions and realities. For example, we desire design to be in the spirit of its time and yet timeless. We want design to serve individual desires while contributing to the common good. We want design to be the product of individual genius and at the same time to be an outgrowth of collaborative synergy. We want design quickly done with care and attention. We desire familiarity and crave novelty. In every design situation, tension provides the necessary inertia to keep the process moving.

Given the volatile nature of these relationships, how does a good design manager handle these opposing forces? One way is explained by Csikszentmihali as the concept of flow (1990). Csikszentmihali describes *flow* as the 'optimal experience'. It is the feeling we get when we perform tasks in a way that removes us from conscious deliberation, with all its corresponding uncertainties and anxieties about doing 'the right thing' in the 'right way'. When in flow, we do not think about what we are doing, we just participate in it. Some of us might experience flow in our work, or when we are engaged in our favorite hobby or sports. To ski down a difficult slope, to let go of our calculating mind and still be in perfect control, but also free to do whatever we desire, is to be in flow. Being fully in the present and losing relationship to time is to be in flow. Csikszentmihali defines flow as a tension. It is a tension between the difficulty of the task and our level of skill. It is also the tension between being in control and letting go. Similar tensions can be found in design innovation. We need to recognize that flow will not emerge merely by letting go of the calculating mind—it is not just a matter of 'letting the force be with you' as portrayed in the popular Star Wars films.

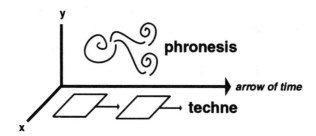

Fig. 10-2 The *x* and *y* of Design

In every design moment, there are two dimensions that have to be dealt with. For convenience we refer to them as the x and the y dimensions (see Fig. 10-2). The *x dimension* has to do with order and the temporal relationships of the activities in the process. It is about

232

how to do things right. This is the dimension dominated by systems thinking as the logic of design. This dimension is related to the idea of *techné*—productive, technical knowledge—in the writings of Aristotle (Dunne, 1993).

To manage the x dimension, a designer needs certain skills like systems thinking. For instance, he or she has to be able to see logical, systemic relationships, especially the relationship between intention and action. To make design work flow, the designer must have the ability to create a stable and creative environment for collaboration and dialogue.

The *y dimension* is related to the idea of *phronesis*—practical, personal knowledge—in the writings of Aristotle (Dunne, 1993). It is nuclear to the designer's ability to make design judgments. It requires a designer to be prepared to take action, to have a well-developed intuition, a perceptive sense of the wholeness of the situation and an ethical and aesthetic appreciation of the design situation. If you think of the x dimension as about doing things in the 'right way', then the y dimension is about doing the 'right thing'. The y dimension is based on the value judgments of the designer.

In the design process, flexibility and control are usually distributed by assigning flexibility to the phronesis dimension and control to the techné side of things. To most people, this seems to be an intuitive and commonsense way to contrast them. It is assumed that to be flexible, the phronesis dimension needs to be weak; that the designer's own values and judgments must be suppressed so as not to hinder the process of adaptive or adoptive change. The feeling is that designers with 'strong' ideals and values are unable to adapt to changing situations and will not be flexible or adaptive. Stability and control, on the other hand, are assumed to be achieved by controlling the techné

233

dimension. This is one reason why designers with a strong, innovative, creative, or idealistic self-image often resist being managed in any way.

Which dimension to focus on is a question of balance and symmetry, not right or wrong or even dominance or equality. Symmetry is an aesthetic concept, in line with Wittgenstein's (1963) sense of 'fit' in a situation. If the phronesis dimension of design is over-emphasized, the techné will automatically be suppressed and vice versa. We believe that either extreme leads to poor conditions for design management.

When the phronesis dimension is the only one given voice, we often wind up with designers who are self-centered, very individualistic, difficult to collaborate with and unpredictable. If the techné dimension is too pronounced, we may find ourselves with an unselfish, objective designer, who collaborates well, but simply focuses on how to do things technically. Such a designer is without his or her own opinions and has a strong need to do things the 'right way'. Neither of these extremes is optimal for design management. Design requires both control and flexibility at the same time.

When we consider that every design process is itself designed, we realize that the overall relationship between the two dimensions is the result of either conscious or unconscious design. Tapping the full potential of the design process requires both dimensions to be fully and equally present. This holistic approach towards composing a design process must be based on a thorough understanding of design. Designing a design process demands even greater insight into the nature of design than that which is required to perform specific design tasks.

Design management is therefore a job for people with extraordinary experience and knowledge of design. To compose and assign design processes is fundamentally a leadership role. It involves creating the right environment, or culture, for design. It requires that the design manager bring the right group of people together, to determine the best possible approach for a specific situation. Design managers are, in effect, designing an ultimate particular design process. One that involves leading people through a complex and risky process in order to evoke the full potential of all involved.

It is important to note at this point that, by definition, production is a transitional phase. By this, we mean that at the end of the production phase there is a transfer of *ownership* from the design team as a whole to the client alone. That is when a design is accepted into the client's world and becomes part of it. The design begins to fulfill its purpose and intent. Up until this point, the design team, in its entirety, has been responsible for the design. The design now becomes the responsibility of the client and the eventual end users; with residual accountability remaining for the entire design team.

Since innovation is about bringing things into the world, it will always be dependent on the design skills and abilities of its production team. These skills and abilities are specific to the field within which the design is taking shape. Often, these skills change over time, as field-specific technology and knowledge is continuously developed. Some aspects of the design process itself are influenced by field-specific conditions. For example, there is a significant difference in the type of detail and specification between an organizational design and an industrial design. Organizational design is primarily people focused, dealing with the details of human cognition and social behavior; while industrial design is primarily engineering focused, dealing with details of technology and industrial processes. As a consequence, without acquiring the skills and experience inherent in your particular trade or craft, you cannot be a competent designer.

Yet, despite these differences, there are foundational and fundamental design principles that transcend specific fields and bind all design thinking together. *The Design Way* is our attempt at presenting a coherent picture of the universal principles of design practice. All designs are brought into the real world through innovation, in a delicate process that cannot be moved forward inattentively or by force. It should now be clear that design production needs to be about *carefulness* and *care taking*.

IV. METAPHYSICS

D esign requires more than a working knowledge of the foundational and fundamental aspects of design. Every designer must also reflect on the substantial metaphysical questions that arise from a design approach to life. These metaphysical issues include: setting the boundaries of design; determining design excellence; ascertaining the designer's responsibility in the outcome of a design; and confronting the inherent good and evil in design. Understanding the metaphysical aspects of design is not optional in a design approach. Competent designers have an obligation to clients, stakeholders, society at large and to themselves to continuously reflect on the meaning and consequences of these themes.

The subjects we will explore in the next three chapters are *the guarantor-of-design, the evil of design* and *the splendor of design*. These metaphysical considerations define significant questions found at the edges of design inquiry.

11. THE GUARANTOR-OF-DESIGN (g.o.d.)

Design is an act of world creation. As such it can be experienced both as inspiring and frightening. As a world creator, the designer can be overwhelmed by questions such as: Do I have the right to cause significant change to the world? What is the right approach to make changes? What kind of changes are good, or just and for whom? As a designer, am I fully responsible and accountable for my designs and to whom? Can I be relieved of responsibility in some way? If not, how can I prepare for this responsibility and assume the liability of being fully accountable for my design judgments and actions?

Today we understand that our designs can dramatically change the conditions of reality experienced by ordinary people. The world is becoming more and more a human artifact, a designed place. To be a designer is therefore to be the creator of new worlds. It is a calling of enormous responsibility, with its concomitant accountability. This is true even if each individual designer is only involved in a very small design act, playing merely a minor part in the totality of the redesigning of an emerging new reality. Our individual designs will always be contributing causes to an overall composition that is an emergent new world.

Given this fact, what is the nature of this ever-renewing world? A world that each designer is, consciously or unconsciously, midwifing into existence through her or his contribution. Is it possible to discern the attributes of good design and to be intentional about evoking their presence in such a complex environment? The only thing we know for sure is that it is impossible to predict with certainty whether a realized design will result in the betterment of human life. We can hope for this, but nothing is absolute before it is realized. Also, we can never know what the unintended consequences of a design will be and whom they will affect, as discussed in our chapter on service. So, with this state of affairs in mind, what is our responsibility, as designers, in co-creating this new world? Do we accept responsibility for our part in world making, and what does that mean for our accountability and liability?

We feel most designers would probably answer that they don't really have any responsibility for the whole—that they can only take responsibility for their small piece of the puzzle. Often, designers feel they are merely agents working for the client, doing what they are told to do in exchange for fair compensation. But are these valid answers? Can there be any valid arguments for making the case that, as a designer, you do not have responsibility for your design in the context of the whole? This thorny question is the topic of this chapter.

For most of us, it would be truly comforting to know with certainty that we are doing good things for the right reasons—that our imagination and creativity lead us to the right conclusions, solutions, ideas and designs within clearly delineated bounds of responsibility. But how can this happen? Is it even possible for a designer to learn how 'to know' in that way? Is there a *guarantor* of good, dependable design judgments, whether designing a life, an artifact, or an organization?

These are difficult questions to answer. We will begin our response by distinguishing between the two kinds of *guarantors* that are involved in design. C. West Churchman used the concept of guarantor as the

240

ninth category in the formulation of his twelve 'categories for planning' (Churchman, 1971, 1979). Churchman stated that:

> I was reminded of Descartes' "Dangerous voyage" of doubt, and his search for a guarantor, and of Kant's vision, in the second Critique of humanity's gradually reconciling virtue and happiness, and the need to postulate a guarantor of this endless search.

C. West Churchman (1979)

At an annual meeting for the Operations Research Society of America, Churchman presented his formulation of the guarantor category that resulted in an arresting response to the concept by one of the attendees:

> ... I gave my luncheon address, which fell unheeded into the pool, except for one ripple. The ripple was Wroe Alderson*, who delighted, suggested a slight addition, "guarantor of destiny"—or, in these days when everything has it acronym, GOD. (*One of the leading authors in marketing during the 1950s.)

C. West Churchman (1979)

Building on this seminal idea, we first consider the *guarantor-of-destiny* (*G.O.D.*) as it is related to design. This is the challenge of discerning the guarantor of human intentions. It is the expected guarantee that choosing to engage in the complex and challenging process of design is a good decision to make, one that will secure the desired improvement in the lives of everyone touched by design. The locus and character of the *guarantor-of-destiny* is the fundamental concern of those who are being served through their participation in the design process—your clients and other stakeholders. It is the foundation

241

upon which they can place their belief that they serve their best interests by choosing to initiate and participate in a design process when they believe it is appropriate to do so.

The purpose of trying to gain some instrumental understanding of the *guarantor-of-destiny* is to find enough certainty and security in humankind's ability to deal intentionally, and successfully, with the deeper issues of life—issues that have been the focus of philosophic and religious discourse through the ages. Issues that are only obliquely confronted in any design process. For example, what does it mean to be human? What is the purpose of our individual and collective lives, to what end? Is the cosmos indifferent to humans, or do we have significance? Is the world an accident of physics, or is it designed? Can there be change by intention, or only as the consequences of chance and necessity? Is this quest for comprehension a reasonable expectation to have? Do we have the right to expect this deeper understanding of others or ourselves? Although they may not be conscious of it, destiny is the foremost implicit issue for clients of design. The *guarantor-of-destiny—G.O.D.*—is an implied contract among all of us, given the unknowns, the unknowable and the uncertainties in the human condition; that what we ought to do is ascertainable, what we try to do is possible and what we can do counts.

Alternatively, we consider the allied idea of a *guarantor-of-design* (*g.o.d.*) that is focused on the legitimacy and certainty of the designer's actions and accountability. In our day-to-day lives as designers, we rarely spend time pondering questions of human destiny. Instead, we tend to deal with particular design situations, involving a particular design process that occurs at a particular place and time, with particular people and resources. Regardless of whether we choose to be aware of them or not, questions of responsibility of outcomes in design decisions, and actions in the particular design situation, cause difficult challenges for designers. They also have significant consequences for clients and other stakeholders. These difficulties lead to the designer's wish for some kind of guarantor, someone or something that can guarantee that the decisions and judgments made are the right ones. This becomes the longing and search for a *guarantor-of-design.*

It seems common for designers, even at the limited level of the particular project or program, to be unwilling to accept full responsibility for the consequences of their designs. This is, in many ways, not surprising, as taking on responsibility can be not only challenging, but also quite dangerous morally, socially and politically as well. To bring this issue of design responsibility to greater light and open it up to reflective dialogue, we will present some common ways designers relieve themselves of accountability for their design decisions. We will argue that these attempts by designers to divorce themselves of responsibility for the ultimate outcomes of their designs cannot be justified and are unacceptable, given the accumulating effect of small designs on the larger design of society.

One of the main ways designers avoid responsibility is by cloaking their actions within the tradition of 'truth-telling'. In this tradition, we do not have to take on any responsibility for unintended outcomes, or for the larger emergent whole, since we are only obeying principles that transcend our individual volition. The only thing we have to be concerned with, is whether or not we possess true knowledge and how we came to acquire it. In this 'truth-telling' tradition, our focus is on appropriate methods of inquiry, controlled techniques of observation and record keeping, which guide us with certainty in our search for

243

reliable truth. This design approach is strikingly similar to the western tradition of scientific inquiry.

Design, however, does not reside restrictively in the realm of the *true*. It lives in the world of the *real* and *ideal* as well (see chapter *The Real*). Within the context of the real and the ultimate particular, we will never be able to find absolute truths that can guide us in our design actions. This is because description and explanation do not prescribe action. Moreover, predication and control do not justify action. As designers, we cannot depend on a source of wisdom outside of ourselves for guidance that will relieve us of our ultimate responsibility. Design decisions are based on judgment and judgment is both personal and situational. In the end, design is always an act of faith.

Sometimes the nature of the real situation can be difficult to handle. It gives the designer a lot of power and authority, which can be both overwhelming and frightening. Overwhelming, when you realize that you can act on the world in such a way as to create significant and irreversible change in other people's lives. Frightening, when people hold you responsible for these changes. Or, more perversely, when not held responsible, you may feel disinclined to take responsibility on your own and become accountable for getting better at what you do, thus perpetuating poor habits of judgment.

There are several additional routes designers use to escape responsibility. These strategies are not necessarily chosen in a conscious and intentional way. They are not tactics used solely by people who lack courage or ethics. These approaches are quite likely very natural reactions to situations where a designer comes face-to-face with mind-numbing complexity and uncertainty, or when the designer is not in possession of enough resources, knowledge, or skill to fulfill the task at hand.

All of these strategies attempt to find some solid and dependable base for design actions. This yearning can be labeled as the search for a *guarantor-of-design*. It is a search that takes on many disguises and can be found in every design field. The search for a *guarantor-of-design* can be understood as a way to reduce the designers' feeling of isolation, which can occur as a result of their assuming sole or primary responsibility for a design. A *guarantor-of-design* constructs a means of measuring design judgments and decisions against some standard of 'good' or 'bad'. This allows the designer to move with confidence through the design process, lending legitimacy to the outcome at the same time.

We are not arguing that every designer is trying to consciously escape responsibility. There are designers who embrace responsibility, not only as something necessary (although problematic), but as a component that gives design a special quality, character and attraction. Responsibility means to be accountable for how one employs power. To be able to use your power to change the world is one of the real wonders of design. But even for those who already embrace responsibility, we believe it is important to reflect on the source, place and nature of responsibility in design.

Often with design teams, communication around the issue of responsibility remains foggy at best. Most of us have met with statements like: "I don't think we have to do that, it's not our responsibility," or "We can't do that, no one told us to." This is why everyone on the design team needs to reflect on what the concept of *guarantor-of-design* means to them, as well as how it relates to colleagues, employers, clients and society as a whole.

245

There are at least three reasons why designers search for a *guarantor-of-design*, each involving a different approach. The first approach involves designers who are trying to *move responsibility*, the second motive is an attempt to *hide responsibility*, and finally some designers hope to *remove responsibility* entirely.

The most common way of avoiding responsibility is to try to restrict the degrees of freedom in the design process, by *moving responsibility* to something outside the control of the designer. This can be done in many different ways. You can move responsibility to the design process itself, or to other people, or to some other guiding principle.

For instance, a designer can use a prescriptive method that guides him or her through the entire design process. The more detailed and rigid the method, the fewer degrees of freedom the designer has access to. A completely controlled and comprehensive method restricts the designer's degrees of freedom fully. It means that the method will be the sole bearer of responsibility. If a designer rigorously follows the method, he or she cannot be blamed for not being rational, or logical. The designer can show that the method was followed and if something is to be judged, it is the method, not the designer. By following this route, the role of the designer has been transformed into something more along the lines of a simple operant.

Another way to move responsibility is to turn to other people for help. A designer can always argue that he or she is only trying to satisfy someone else. It could be a client, a customer, a stakeholder, or a user. The designer can ask any one of these people for help in the process, in a way that relieves him or her of responsibility. If the designer always lets other people decide on choices and solutions, responsibility will, by default, be removed from his or her shoulders.

Unfortunately, at the same time, the designer's skill and specific knowledge also disappears, since the designer has stopped being the person that creates the new and the unexpected. When a designer is only producing what other people want, or have decided on, that designer has simply become a facilitator.

Shifting responsibility by any of the above means is not, necessarily, problematic or bad. These strategies can be part of a conscious design decision. In no case, though, is it possible to practice design—as an authentic designer—if responsibility has been removed by any of these options. When responsibility is removed from the designer, the role of the designer is transformed into something else.

The last point we would like to make about moving responsibility is that it still leaves a situation where responsibility is visible and open to judgments: the only change being that the designer is no longer the target for accountability. Another approach is to *hide responsibility*, or at least to hide it from inspection. This approach can happen in any number of ways. We will discuss a few here. We have dubbed these forms of hiding responsibility the *internal, external* and *administrative slough-off*.

As an artist, a designer can argue that the design is a result of an internal force, such as intuition, or a feeling that is beyond the control of the designer—the *internal slough-off*. A designer who uses this approach often trusts this nebulous internal stimulus as a reliable source and uses it as a *guarantor-of-design*. Expressions such as "I trust my intuition," "Let your feelings guide your way," or "Just follow your heart," are common. These internal sources of inspiration cannot, by definition, be inspected by the designer—or by anyone else. Using this platform, the designer argues that he or she only did what had to be done in response to these internal sources. Since these sources are situated beyond the reach of our conscious, reflective mind, we cannot analyze, inspect, or influence them and, therefore, cannot judge them. The designer acts only as a conduit, a spokesman, or a messenger, for his or her inner inspiration.

By looking to the spiritual, the designer can find external sources of guidance—the *external* or *spiritual slough-off*. A spiritual source can be used as a *guarantor-of-design* for almost any kind of design process. We can count on this source to provide us with insights, ideas and guidance and, as a soothing consequence, peace of mind. A spiritual approach is used to see things in a different way, or to be able to interpret reality in a more true or ideal way. To let yourself be a channel for a spiritual mandate shields you from responsibility as a designer, which makes the rationale behind your design actions very difficult for anyone else to inspect or analyze. This can be the whispering of the muses, the demands of selfish genes, the commands of a personal God, or the manipulations of evil spirits—i.e., 'the devil made me do it'. In extreme cases, this can lead to situations where the designer ceases to be an individual, or independent entity and becomes essentially part of something transcendent of the human realm—something impossible to hold accountable to mere human agency.

One of the easiest ways to hide responsibility is to imbed all actions in a complex, administrative web of responsibilities and authority relationships—the *administrative slough-off*. When this web becomes convoluted enough, it's practically impenetrable; it is impossible to tell what consequence resulted from what cause and which decisions affected what actions. This effectively stops anyone from knowing whose ideas are actually being manifested in the design. The administrative approach is often more accidental than it is intentional. In many design processes, we end up in an administrative situation no one really wanted or planned for and responsibility just seems to evaporate into a web of contorted relations. With this slough-off, the individual designer may still act as a piecemeal designer, but—in relationship to the overall design process—it is now impossible to know who is responsible.

As was the case with moving responsibility, hiding responsibility is not necessarily problematic or bad. Although the strategy of moving responsibility is often deliberate, the hiding process seems to be more unintentional. Frequently, it is simply a consequence of many diverse decisions being made in a helter-skelter fashion, regarding how the design process should be carried out.

When a designer can convincingly show that the result of a design process is based on something that is not negotiable, or subjective, but is, instead, something truly universal—responsibility has been effectively removed. This can be done in a number of ways, but some approaches are more common than others.

A popular approach is to use the scientific method. Scientifically derived truth, as the *guarantor-of-design*, is one way to say that the process cannot end in any way other than the one prescribed by the universal laws of logic and reason. When the design process is guided by scientific truth, the correct design will always be determined in relationship to nature and natural laws. Nature is the container of all answers; if we obey the rules dictated by nature, we cannot be accused of making the wrong kind of design decisions.

Another approach is to use the principle of ecological sustainability as the most appropriate guide for decision-making. If nature's design is taken as a given—and we humans have no right to question or change the natural order of things—then, everything we design has to be in full accord with the way nature requires things to be. The only responsibility the designer has is to maintain, or preserve, nature's naturally ordered design.

Even in the absence of universal, scientific truths, or some template of nature's own design, one can find belief systems that provide the means to remove responsibility. In these cases, the designer only acts in accordance with something larger, truer, or nobler, than any set of criteria that may emerge from a specific client's expressed needs.

When all else fails, designers can simply use the logic of harsh, everyday reality as an argument for not assuming responsibility. "I can only do so much!" a designer might wail. In this case, he or she feels constrained by a concrete, real-world situation and, therefore, claims that his or her design outcome is not a matter of choice or volition. Here, we're letting chance and fate be our *guarantor-of-design*.

All of these choices can generally be seen as attempts to restrict the degrees of freedom in a design practice. But, they differ significantly in how they operate in practice and the types of assumptions they make about the role of the designer. There is no simple answer to the question: "Who should have responsibility in design and how should this responsibility be put in operation?" This question will continue to elude us, just as we will never know the exact difference between the particular and the true. We will never find an absolute, or universally correct, answer. But we believe it's possible to argue that based on our definition of what good design is, if you want to be a good designer—there are no justifiable ways to move, hide, or remove responsibility for your own actions.

Given our very busy lives, we often want to minimize our efforts and the energy necessary to accomplish things we need done. We try to find ways to make things happen without our complete attention. This is also true in design. Since design is very demanding and basically very personal, it takes a lot of intellectual energy. If we are afraid of doing the wrong thing in a design process, it is only natural that we search for ways to reduce the need for energy and personal engagement while attending to this concern.

But there is no *guarantor-of-design* 'out there' that allows us to conserve personal energy and minimize focused attention. None of the approaches described above are valid candidates for such a guarantor. Design is about creating a new reality, and there are no givens in that process. There are no theories, methods, techniques, or tools that can calculate, predict or envision the truly best future reality. The true future does not exist as a predetermined, objective fact. As human beings, we have the capacity to create a different future—restricted only by our present reality and our imagination.

So, given that responsibility can never be escaped, where does this leave us? Can we find a *guarantor-of-design* anywhere? We argue that, in fact, it is possible only through the development of one's own *design character*.

A designer's character is his or her core. No judgment made by a designer can be made solely based on comprehensive knowledge. Judgments always depend on the designer's core values as first introduced in the *Judgment* chapter. Design judgment, in this sense, is an act of faith. The designer has to believe in his or her capacity to make good judgments. In design, we find many kinds of judgments, all with their roots grounded in the character of the designer. It is a question of a designer's whole being. As a consequence, this leaves us in a place where we must consider the designer to be a self-reflective individual, with a fully developed character. This character manifests itself

251

through design tasks, illuminating the designer's values, beliefs, skills, sensibility, reason, ethics and aesthetics.

Thus, designers must learn to accept design responsibility as something integral to each designer's character. But how can we reduce the stress and worry designers invariably feel regarding this responsibility? We think that the more a designer understands the real nature of design, the better he or she can deal with the responsibility of design. This, in turn, actually enhances the joy of creating new designs. When a designer truly realizes his or her ability and skills, as well as shortcomings, he or she can deal with the dilemmas of responsibility, but only in the way dilemmas can be dealt with—by learning to live with them.

This is in line with the reasoning of Martha Nussbaum, when she argues that we need education that liberates students. When this is done, we get students that "have looked into themselves and developed the ability to separate mere habit and convention from what they can defend by argument" (Nussbaum, 1997). Not only will this help students to become more personally accountable in their creative work, it also allows them to "have ownership of their own thought and speech, and this imparts to them a dignity that is far beyond the outer dignity of class and rank." Nussbaum argues that this is the only way to cultivate students that will not be uncritical, moral relativists. For her, ownership of one's own mind yields understanding that "some things are good and some bad, some defensible and others indefensible."

The same is true for designers. We must nourish our own dignity of mind in order to develop the necessary ability to make advanced design judgments, at our own skill level, within any unique situation. In order for this to happen, designers need to develop a strong

252

character. We agree with Nussbaum that it is possible to "teach them how to argue, rigorously and critically, so that they can call their minds their own."

Robert Nozick (1989) states that, to create character, we have to live the *examined life*. His basic argument is similar to Nussbaum's and seems to argue against the idea of an external guarantor. He writes: "When we guide our lives by our own pondered thoughts, it is our life that we are living, not someone else's." According to Nozick and Nussbaum, to be good designers, we must base our design actions and judgments on our own core character.

Now, how does one learn to trust, or even know, one's own core character? We can do this by constantly examining our practice and our thoughts. Donald Schön describes this examination as two types of reflection; reflection-in-action and reflection-on-action (Schön, 1983). Reflection-in-action is a first-order reflective process that focuses on each judgment or action taken in the process of our designing something in particular. Reflection-on-action is a second-order reflective process that involves stepping back from any immediate judgment making that takes place within a specific design process, in order to focus reflectively on the process of our design behavior in general.

It is an approach in line with the ideas of James Hillman, when he discusses *character* and *calling* (Hillman, 1996). He argues that a person's character has a calling. In order to fully live, you have to live in accordance with your calling. In design terms, we interpret this to mean that each individual is developing into a unique designer and has to form his or her design character in line with his or her calling. This can't be done if character development is neglected, in hopes of discovering an external guarantor. Hillman's book on character presents an extremely rich picture on what developing a character can be understood to be.

So, once again, we are led to the conclusion that there is no justification for an external *guarantor-of-design*, even if there is a felt need. We believe designers must accept responsibility for all they design. This accountability should be an integral part of our character. We should be relied on to fulfill obligations, not only to our clients, but also to a higher authority, one that is concerned for the sake of others and the environment in which we live.

This added requirement is not meant to restrain a designer's ability to design, but to improve the designer's capacity to create better designs that will, in turn, have fewer unintended or undesirable outcomes. Any negative consequences the designer incurs by accepting her or his design responsibilities can be mitigated through better education and professional training.

In terms of education, we believe that there is a big difference between knowledge *in* design and knowledge *about* design. To know how to design does not necessarily mean that the designer has a well-developed understanding of design and of the role of being a designer. To have a good understanding *of* design is the first step towards developing a mature design character.

Reflecting on responsibility, as we have done in this chapter, is one way of better understanding design. If this is taken seriously, it will provide the designer with the intellectual tools needed to make visible in design the issues of responsibility, thus triggering further dialogue and reflective thought.

Knowing how people move, hide, or remove responsibility, we can start to evaluate our own habits and preferences. Students or professional designers can easily do this while they engage in design on different projects. A close analysis of how responsibility is accounted for will show not only the complexity of the issue, but may also reveal outlets through which we can deal with responsibility in open and constructive ways

This increased willingness to accept responsibility, on the part of the designer, requires that society also step up to the plate, by not wielding vindictive, fault-based responses, but instead, by sharing in the ultimate responsibility for design outcomes.

Now, more than ever, there is a need for serious dialogue on design responsibility; especially given the speed with which we are designing new hard and soft technologies that radically change the foundations and realities of society, as we know it. Even if each individual designer's creation is not primarily responsible for the totality of the changes brought by new designs, that totality is an emergent consequence of each small design's contribution. Therefore, every designer plays an important and significant part in the overall designed world in which we all live.

12. THE EVIL OF DESIGN

D esign is often paradoxical (see Fig. 12-1). Qualities that may appear to be opposites from a single vantage point, are actually different dimensions of the same complex set of design relationships. Just as it is impossible to take in all views of a building at once (you must move around and through its architecture to see all sides of it), it is impossible to see the whole of anything in a design from just one perspective. In design, when one attribute is revealed, another may suddenly be hidden from sight. But the fact that you are no longer aware of the second attribute does not mean it has disappeared from the composition. In fact, a wide variety of contradictory design attributes can be present at the same time, as the following list will attest.

- DESIGN IS NON-ATTACHMENT AND TOTAL ENGAGEMENT
- DESIGN IS FLUX AND PERMANENCE
- DESIGN IS KNOWING AND NAIVETE
- DESIGN IS EXPERIENCE AND FRESH EYES
- DESIGN IS COLLABORATION AND SOLITUDE
- DESIGN IS PROCESS AND STRUCTURE
- DESIGN IS CYCLIC AND EPISODIC
- DESIGN IS CONTROL AND UNCONTROLLABLE
- DESIGN IS UNIQUE AND UNIVERSAL
- DESIGN IS INFINITE AND FINITE
- DESIGN IS TIMELESS AND TEMPORAL
- DESIGN IS SPLENDOR AND EVIL

Fig. 12-1 Paradoxes of Design

257

Paradoxical relationships are more common than we would like to admit. They are, in fact, an essential nature of the human experience. Life is complex and tensional. These tensions between apparent opposites, such as joy and sorrow, are usually perceived as abnormal in the science-dominated Western tradition. This tradition holds that resolved truth, especially objectively resolved truth, is of the highest value. Indeed, from this perspective, resolved truth becomes the only outcome worth seriously pursuing.

Tension is regarded as something to be resolved, rather than valued; paradoxes are looked upon as relationships that must be 'fixed', in favor of one or the other member of a tensional pair. When one side of the pair 'wins', tension is released and there is a loss of aesthetic quality, almost a sense of flatness, or lack of depth. It is what we sense when we seriously contemplate utopias and master plans. If everything is in agreement, following a consensual path, the excitement of human differences—held in breathtaking tension—is lost, along with what is most exciting about engaging in life at its fullest.

Good design's most interesting paradox is that it is both wondrous and evil. This is not the same pairing of apparent opposites as the more common duality of good and evil. We are not talking about Evil, with a capital E, designating malevolent forces dedicated to the destruction of everything that is good in the world, or counter to the positive presence of God. It is true that design has been considered Evil in this way. Some designs have been attributed to the work of the devil or the influence of Evil spirits. For instance, a European bishop banned the use of rifled barrels on guns, because the resulting superior accuracy over the old, smooth bore muskets could only be due to the intervention of the devil.

258

Consideration of the concept of evil in human affairs has not been the focus of modern thinkers, outside of those associated with religious traditions. Historically evil has been considered from many perspectives, including spiritual, social and political. This includes many of the dominant religions of the West, which define evil as disobedience of God's authority; as disorder and that which creates disorder; as abominations, malevolence, sin and vice. Concepts of evil from secular perspectives have even included willfulness, cruelty, irrationality, waywardness, conflict, immorality, crime, sociopathology and ultimately the banal cruelty of everyday life (Rorty, 2001).

One of the traditional definitions of evil concerns that which breaks unity and separates the individuated self from the ultimate prime causal principle of the All, which is a seminal aspect of the 'perennial philosophy'. Within this framework, evil in a large number of spiritual traditions has been identified with a separation from the one, absolute and supreme Nature (Huxley, 1944). Aldous Huxley points out that spiritual traditions throughout time consider evil as any division of this Unity, beginning with the concept of duality, the first step in the deconstruction of the ultimate Whole. This separation can be detected in the dividing out of 'self' through reasoning, will and feeling from the whole.

These attributes are manifest in our definition of evil in design. Design is evil when that which is not desired but which, nevertheless, has been made manifest because of design activity—whether by *chance*, *necessity*, or *intention*—becomes part of the world. To a lesser degree, evil in design is something that disrupts balance, harmony, order and other meaning making attributes of human existence. Design can be considered evil even by some of the earliest definitions of evil, such as breaking a taboo, or going beyond the territorial boundaries of the tribe. In every case, evil is not merely the absence of something desired, but in addition, it is the presence of something immensely unsettling.

Even when the splendor of a particular design is clearly apparent and bears witness to the best of human potential, that design often has aberrant outcomes, in addition to those expected from a good solution. Unintended, systemic consequences of an innovated design make themselves visible in both the near and long term. These consequences arise out of not knowing enough about the complexity of the design context prior to designing, and not understanding enough about the dynamics of introducing a new set of relationships or variables into a complex environment. Designers, in their rational persona, imagine that this situation can be improved by just learning more about the nature of complex realities. However, there are some outcomes that cannot be mitigated through more knowledge or more information. It is impossible to be comprehensive in the acquisition of knowledge, particularly design knowledge. Judgments are always made in the absence of perfect knowledge, and there are always surprises when changes are made in the real world. It is impossible to predict and control every outcome of a design intervention made in the context of a complex, particular situation.

There are certain qualities of design that can only be considered as evil in light of all the variety of ways that evil has been defined throughout the ages. It's also true that some of these evil outcomes are considered to be inevitable, necessary and unavoidable. Below, you will find three categories of evil that can be present in any design. This classification helps to build a conceptual framework for reflective consideration in a design approach (see Fig. 12-2).

NECESSITY—NATURAL EVIL

GOING BEYOND BOUNDARIES

NATURAL ORDER OF LIFE—SURVIVAL AT ANY COST

LOST OPPORTUNITIES

LOST ALTERNATIVES

POINT OF VIEW

NATURAL FORCE

CHANCE—ACCIDENTAL EVIL

POWER WITHOUT UNDERSTANDING

CAUSE WITHOUT CONNECTION

MISFORTUNE AND ACCIDENTS

BREAKDOWN OF NATURAL ORDER

INTENTION—WILLFUL EVIL

DESTROYING LIFE AND LIFE-GIVING ESSENCE

POWER WITHOUT CHARITY

AGENCY WITHOUT COMMUNITY

DOMINANCE OVER OTHERS

USING OTHERS AS A MEANS ONLY

SEPARATION FROM UNITY

Fig. 12-2 Categories of Evil in Design with Examples

Our first category is *natural evil*, which is always an integral part of the process of change, including the types of changes wrought by design. This is a form of evil that is a necessary and an unavoidable part of all life. In any creative act, something new is brought into the world at the expense of the old—which is then destroyed. There may be good and necessary reasons for the change brought on by design, but that does not deny the real and painful experience of grief and emptiness, brought by the loss of that which has been replaced.

By definition, any design is an act going beyond established boundaries. This is also one of the oldest definitions of evil. In most cases, everyday designing isn't considered 'boundary-crossing' because those boundaries that such designs do cross are too weak to be thought of as strong norms, in the same sense as a taboo, for example. Moreover, these boundaries are usually not even visible as boundaries for behavior. Those designs and designers, that are seen as causing changes that affect the normal routine of life, however, are often treated with a certain amount of irritation, if not outright hostility. This is because they have crossed the boundary maintaining the defined limits of normal or typical everyday activity. This form of design evil can be perilous to the designer, because even if the change is for the benefit of those affected, the designer is still cast as an enemy of people's peace of mind and routine existence.

A new design brings a shadow with it. There are always unintended consequences associated with design, many of which are negative. This is related to another, more obvious natural evil—the loss of opportunities. When a design is brought into the world and made real, its very presence excludes other opportunities. The substantial investment of money, energy, material and time into a new design directly excludes other attempts to make an alternative design. This also holds true for more abstract investments, such as pride and status. This is because identity and self-image become invested in a commitment to the new reality emerging as a consequence of the new design's meaning making presence. This form of evil is closely related to the 'survival-at-any-cost' strategy of evolution. Even though it appears this strategy is the essence of nature, in our human vocabulary, it carries the suspicion of being an evil that needs to be seriously redeemed.

New designs also bring with them specific points of view that define them as evil because of our human frame of reference. The material, corporeal world forms the substance of design, yet this realm is considered evil by many spiritual traditions. Humans are encouraged to avoid focusing on this aspect of life, yet it is the very material from which a designer assembles his or her design palette. Associated with this perspective of evil is the old and enduring notion that evil is a natural and eminent force in the affairs of people: one must continually balance and compensate for the effect of this unrelenting evil energy that's always at work in the natural order of things.

Our second category is *accidental evil*. This type of design evil can be thought of as avoidable. Some examples are: power without understanding, agency without interrelationship (i.e., acting without personal connection to consequences), the misfortune of being in the wrong place at the wrong time as a matter of mischance, bad luck, or tragedy. This form of evil happens out of ignorance, carelessness, or inattention and is not the outcome of an intention to do harm. For example, the design of toys that are actually dangerous for children is the consequence of inattention to those being served. Accidental evil can be modified, or mitigated, by becoming more fully informed and aware when engaging in design. Good design judgments are dependent on having the right design knowledge, but that's not all. Design knowledge cannot be separated from the 'knower'. Therefore, in design, character counts. This is similar to the way that good character counts in making wise decisions, in the absence of a predetermined

263

outcome. This is a concept known as phronesis, as introduced in the *Production and Care Taking* chapter. Good design is dependent on good designers as much as the best information or know-how.

Finally, there is the category of *willful evil*. In a design context, this includes power without charity and agency without community—i.e., acting on people's behalf without their contractual consent to do so. It also includes dominance over others; including collective dominance over the individual, individual dominance over the collective and dominance of one individual over another. It involves the use of people as a means only rather than an end in themselves. Finally, it includes the destruction of human life and life-giving essence.

These are just a few examples of intentional evil that can become a part of design. The history of human affairs is filled with designs that were evil by intention, such as those created by Albert Speer, the German architect, who among other things created organizational designs based on slave labor for the Nazis during the Second World War. A more recent example is the design of Web-based technology that intrudes on unsuspecting users of the World Wide Web. This design shields the identity of all those involved in the creation and utilization of Web-based child pornography sites. Powerful design theories and approaches can be used in the creation of things, concrete or abstract, that history will hold as evil in the most literal sense, such as the design of nuclear weapons, that was considered defensible in its time.

Becoming good at design, or helping others to become good at design, does not assure that good design will be the outcome. The theories and practices of design are still subject to the willfulness of the human being. We as humans are not bound to proscriptions of character that guarantee our good intentions as well as magnificent designs. That challenge is well beyond the scope of this book, but it is an essential consideration.

ACCEPT CHALLENGE OF DESIGN
NO RIGHT ANSWERS
NO GIVENS
NOT COMPREHENSIVE

ACCEPT POWER OF DESIGN
CREATE REAL WORLD

ACCEPT RESPONSIBILITY OF DESIGN
SERVICE TO OTHER

ACCEPT ACCOUNTABILITY OF DESIGN
EVIL OF DESIGN
GUARANTOR-OF-DESIGN
ARTIFACT EVOKES OWN REALITY

ACCEPT PARADOXES OF DESIGN
BOTH/AND/NEITHER

ACCEPT DISCIPLINE OF DESIGN
SKILL
AUTHENTIC ENGAGEMENT
FOCUS
LIMITS

ACCEPT POTENTIAL OF DESIGN
EVOKE THE SUBLIME
CREATE THE BEAUTIFUL
CAUSE INTENTIONAL REALITY
SECURE THE ETHICAL AND JUST
BEGIN WITH INFINITE POSSIBILITIES
SERVE BASIC FUNCTIONAL NEEDS AND EXPECTATIONS

Fig. 12-3 Accepting Challenges of Design

How is it possible to become a designer and accept design, as a legitimate human activity that ought to be supported and developed by the larger human enterprise—when evil is intimate to the whole enterprise? A wise next step is to embrace the essential nature of design and prepare accordingly. This includes resolutely accepting design's most uncertain, contradictory, dangerous and promising challenges (see Fig. 12-3).

The splendor of design reaches beyond the grasp of the potential and actual consequences of evil. We truly can create the sublime, despite imperfect designers and a dangerous world. Design can accommodate the hopes and aspirations of every human being, even given strict limits and imperfections. Human nature is such that it is completely natural—not unnatural—to take on the challenge of co-creating the world. And human designers must do this by fully participating in the tension that results from the struggle between good and evil in our very real world. This is why it is so important that we create a design culture to act as a crucible for this intense work.

13. THE SPLENDOR OF DESIGN

We live in a world of designed artifacts, some concrete and others abstract. Together with the natural world, these designs (whether things, systems, processes, or symbols) make up the whole of our reality. It is a reality populated by both the beautiful and the ugly, the good and bad and sometimes even the dangerous. Every day, we use—or struggle with—designs of every shape and size. Some of them we love, some we endure, others we hate, but most of them, we never even notice. They just exist as a natural part of our lives.

But sometimes a design becomes the conveyor of *soul*. Soul is an animating essence, an essential quality of a holistic composition. We are struck by the power of such a design—by its beauty, integrity and usefulness. We marvel at the way it bestows meaning and value on itself and its environment. As a designer, measuring our own steps along the design path, this is what we are always striving to create—designs that emanate *soul*, that are part of something unbound by time, place and material.

How do we distinguish those designs that are merely stylish or fashionable from those that express levels of excellence that reach into the realm of soul? What is the process by which we experience, evaluate and judge our designs? What is it that makes us experience designs as bad and ugly, or authentic and soulful? Consciously and unconsciously, we are in evaluative relationships with the designs making up our reality. The forms these types of discerning judgment take are not always obvious. Given the importance of this mindfulness, we will spend some time trying to understand how we connect appreciatively to the world, specifically the artificial world that we ourselves are responsible for having created (Janlert & Stolterman, 1997).

Hillman (1996) argues that one way to broker an understanding is to entertain the idea that our environments—physical, social and cultural—include all the attending material forms that are, or can be, conveyors of soul. They are *ensouled*. Such a view has crucial consequences for anybody who wishes to be a designer. First of all, how is it possible, for an all too human designer, to ensoul a design? Secondly, why is it important to judge design in this way, using such loaded concepts as 'soul' and 'ensoulment'? Isn't it sufficient to evaluate designs in the context of quality or excellence?

We don't think so. Quality is not robust enough as a scale of measurement against which to judge good design. At least not if the ambition is to create designs that will have a positive impact on our reality, including how we affirmatively occupy that reality—an ambition to create designs that are of consequence in the emergent course of human destiny. The way people assess the value and worth of designs can't be fully spelled out by simply using concrete concepts, such as appearance, efficiency, usefulness, functionality, etc. We need appreciative measurements that can capture the richness of the whole design; for example, in terms of aesthetic responses like love and hate; or the sublime and the beautiful; or the allure of the seamless interface of a design that fits perfectly into a specific context.

Functionality, efficiency, cleverness, usefulness, or whatever measurement we can come up with, doesn't capture, in totality, the way people relate to a design. It must also be valued and judged by the *experience it evokes* and by the aesthetic nature of the design as a *whole*. This has to do with composition, with balance and the relationship

268

between all possible aspects of the design, as introduced in the *Composition* chapter.

We are not talking about superficial aestheticism here. The meaning and value of a design is taken in as a feeling of being deeply *moved* and as a consequence, a feeling of being significantly changed. When we encounter a design's soul, our basic assumptions and world-views are most likely to be challenged. Something profound happens to us as a consequence of our meeting a design at the level of its soul. Our understanding of the world, of our own place in it and our core judgments, all are changed.

For instance, when we encounter a famous building that has survived over centuries and has become symbolic of a culture and civilization, we may, if we give our full attention, become over-whelmed by the depth and strength of its design. Or, we might find ourselves in an organization so well designed that we take immense pleasure from just being part of it. Or, we touch the fine work of a skilled craftsman and feel the delicate balance between form and material that leads to exquisite beauty. Sometimes, in situations like this, we get the feeling that such a design could not have been differ-ent. We might even feel that it is nearly the perfect design. When we are in the presence of a design bearing soul, we glimpse the *splendor of design*. We are captured by the realization that design is about the creation of a soulful world.

What a remarkable challenge—to aid in the ensoulment of the world! But, given this as the Holy Grail, we have to accept that most of the time we will not reach this ideal. In most instances, we are designing for everyday use, hoping to achieve everyday quality. We are under the pressure of restrictions, such as time, material, resources and, as always, money. Still, we know that even in the most circum-

269

scribed and restricted design situation, there might be a design that will turn out to have all the qualities and attributes of the excellence we strive for. In our thousands of endeavors, there just might arise a composition, a choice of material, a never-used symmetry, a combination of human skills and non-human artifacts that will reveal a fundamental new understanding, an emergence of soulfulness, breaking open any previous restrictions.

What is it that gives a design that special character of wholeness and integrity? We all know how hard it is to discuss quality and taste. It is frequently assumed that quality is something entirely subjective—i.e., "Beauty is in the eye of the beholder." It is just as often agreed that taste can not be judged or defined in any general way. However, there are others who propose just the opposite; that quality can be defined without any reference to a specific subject of evaluation. In some aesthetic and art traditions, general definitions of what constitutes both acceptable quality and good taste are asserted. This hangs the discussion concerning quality on a very old and engaging question. That is, where does quality reside—in the object or in the subject?

There are at least three ways to answer this question (Nozick, 1989). There is, according to Robert Nozick, the egoistic stance, the relational stance and the absolute stance. The egoistic stance sees the primary location of value as within the self and things are valued because they are beneficial to the self. The relational stance sees the primary location of value in relations, or connections, as lying primarily between the self and things outside of the self. The third stance locates value as an independent domain such that the things that have value are independent of us. This is very similar to the way

270

in which Robert Pirsig structured the issue of the nature of quality from a technologic and philosophic perspective (Pirsig, 1981)

We will not elaborate on these three stances, but only note that as Nozick shows: when we embrace one stance, we have also, by default, decided how we ourselves—as parts of reality—will be valued. For example, in the egoistic stance we are only the 'means' in someone else's reality. This is true even in our own reality, where we use ourselves to achieve some end; perhaps attaining a high salary that may in fact be harmful to our own health and welfare in the process. The self cannot have priority over all other parts of reality. The other two stances have their merits and problems as well. But most importantly, Nozick asks how it is possible to integrate the three stances.

For a designer, the philosophical situation is even more complicated, since we not only have to consider our own appraisal and valuation approaches to design, but also that of our clients. As designers, we do not stand in isolation from the reality we hope to design. We do our work in close relationship with other people, who may have completely different values and preferences. In the design approach, it is obvious that none of Nozick's three stances, even if integrated, will solve our problem easily. Although any examination of his stances may not be enough to answer the question of where quality resides, it at least gives us a place to start. It helps to eliminate any trivializing attempts to answer the question, which neglect the richness and complexity of the issue by making too many simplifications.

So, as a starting point in our examination of ensoulment, we'll begin with the concepts of *value* and *meaning*. These concepts define two of a myriad of dimensions that can denote the quality of reality. These translate into two of design's most important aspects—the

271

intrinsic value of the design itself—value—and the value of the design in relation to something larger—meaning (Nozick, 1989). It is important to note that from a philosophical viewpoint this is fairly controversial. We will still use this distinction, however, not for a philosophical purpose but as a good way to help designers think about the nature of design. So, in our context, it is being used only as an aid for reflective thought and is not a philosophical assertion.

Let's jump into our discussion of value by noting that all designs have their own intrinsic value. This intrinsic value is what you are taught to recognize and evaluate in an art appreciation class, or a literature class, or during a wine tasting, etc. When we are shown how different components are interrelated, how structure, form, material, texture, smell, taste, etc., fit into the overall theme or purpose of the thing we are evaluating, we learn to see and appreciate the intrinsic value of the design itself. To be a collector of something is a typical way of learning to discern, understand and appreciate subtleties in a design. Through the guidance of colleagues, books and magazines, a collector is slowly learning to pay close attention, to be *sensitive* towards the value of a design (Löwgren & Stolterman, 1999).

This intrinsic value is captured in an integrated and unified whole sometimes called the *organic unity*. Nozick claims that "Something has intrinsic value to the degree that it is organically unified. Its organic unity is its value." The intrinsic value is one reason why we may actually appreciate a specific building, or organization, even though we do not like what the object or system stands for, or how it is used. Even a pacifist may see and value the Pentagon, as a building, even if he or she is completely against its underlying principles.

Just as creating a soulful design takes time and energy, so does the process of sincere *valuing*. To value something means to stand in close relation to it. This is why people react strongly against those who dismiss their favorite design (be it a book, music, food, building, or game) without close examination and attention.

In the design approach, we are not defining value as necessarily dependent on a context or larger system. In reality, however, this is not the typical situation. In fact, it is quite often the opposite. We are typically quite bad at evaluating things that make up our reality based solely on their intrinsic value. More often, we take a much more intentional, or purpose-oriented, approach in our process of evaluating designs. We expect them not only to have value, but also to be useful, to be relevant—i.e., to be meaningful. We want our lives to have meaning. Since we have defined value as residing within a design's own boundaries, meaning then involves connection(s) across those boundaries.

A design has *meaning* when we can see how it is connected to other things that we value. This may lead to an infinite regression, as it is always possible to ask what is the meaning of each new thing, or level we connect to the design. Nozick suggests two ways to stop this regression of meaning making—one is through religion, which leads to a point where we are not allowed to ask further for meaning, e.g., "What is the meaning of God?" The other way is to connect only to the intrinsic value of something that does not have meaning by definition.

This leads us to an alternative situation where value and meaning have a very intricate relationship. In this case, the meaning of an object can be ascertained by linking it with something of value, and something of value can gain meaning by being linked to something else of value. What really makes the difference is the nature of the linkage.

273

The greater the link, the closer, the more forceful, the more intense and extensive it is, the greater the meaning gotten. The tighter the connection with value, the greater the meaning. This tightness of connection means that you are interrelated with the value in a unified way; there is more of an organic unity between you and the value. Your connection with the value, then, is itself valuable; and meaning is gotten through such a valuable connection with value.

R. Nozick (1989)

This examination of value and meaning gives us a chance to see the difficulty of evaluating designs. We cannot evaluate a design only through its intrinsic value, or only through its connective meaning—there is also the relationship between them that must be taken into account (see Fig. 13-1). It is important—at this juncture—to understand that the way these concepts are defined presupposes a static reality. In real life our perception of reality, as well as our knowledge of reality, constantly changes. This also changes our preconditions for both seeing and evaluating the value and meaning of a design, as the conditions for making such judgments are constantly changing.

Value and meaning, as defined above, do not fully account for, or illustrate, what it is that makes a design soulful. Widening our discussion with more abstract conceptualizations would bring us closer to a full understanding of ensoulment, but at the same time, would carry us too far away from the integrative thinking about design that we have tried to focus on in this book. Rather, we will stop here and define the appearance of soul in a design *as an emergent event that is made possible*

274

when value and meaning in a design are in resonance with a particular situation (i.e., when it is a holistic composition).

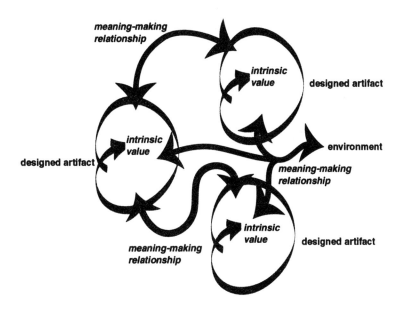

Fig. 13-1 Value and Meaning Making in Design

A design with a strong interconnection between value and meaning entertains the necessary conditions for our recognition of it as a conveyor of a soul. In this sense, soul is the animating essence of the original unifying design parti. It denotes a design that has both intrinsic value and relational meaning. We experience this form of soul when we encounter a design with a unified coherence, in relationship to something giving it meaning. Such a design is sometimes described as having 'integrity' and 'wholeness'; or of being 'rich', 'deep' and 'authentic'. All of these words point to the fact that such a design has a depth and complexity that are not easily revealed. Value is not something that you can easily see without effort. It takes preparation, combined with experience, to reach the point where a designer has enough skill to recognize and appreciate intrinsic value. The same prerequisites exist for the discernment of meaning, as well.

Even if a design possesses value and meaning in some measure, this will not necessarily assure the presence of soul. If the design does not fit faultlessly into its specific situation, we will not be able to experience its soul. If the design is 'ahead of its time', or doesn't make its debut at the right place and the right time, we will—despite its value and meaning—not be able to recognize it fully. We might be able to appreciate its value and separately, its meaning, but if it's not a unified whole, it will lack the valence for the habitation of soul. In addition, it must be in resonance with its context.

As explained in the *Composition* chapter, all designs are compositions. Composition is recognized by qualities of *emergence*. These qualities are often aesthetic in nature but can be ethical and spiritual as well. The appearance of soul is an emergent essence of composition, the same as character is an emergent quality. In order to understand the concept of emergence and its many manifestations, including ensoulment, it is necessary to better understand composition in relationship to the appearance of soul and character.

A soulful design is composed within a specific setting; a context and environment. In most design fields, it takes a skilled designer to recognize and value a composition. But, in other, more everyday situations, we can recognize the composition of a building, for instance, even if we are not architects. We may become upset when someone tries to change the exterior of a building, by replacing

276

windows in a manner that destroys the proportions and the concept of the building. We might react similarly when courses are changed in a program of study in a way that does not reflect the unifying composition of the curriculum. Most of us easily recognize these kinds of compositional changes. Sometimes we do not object, since the composition may still hold together and give us a sense of the whole.

A composition is about details and relations, wholeness and integrity—in effect, it is about giving presence to those things that evoke soul. Composition is very much the emergent quality of a system's unifying essence, in the same way that soul and character are emergent qualities of composition. Therefore, it is not made visible without effort. Every detail in the system contributes to its overall composition, but the composition is transcendent of the details. The structures, functions and forms constituting a design, in compositional relationships with the appropriate context and purpose, set the stage for the emergence of transcendent qualities and attributes. How a designer combines and proportions all of these elements determines whether the composition is strong or weak; whether it will, to a greater or lesser degree, succeed or fail.

It is not easy to find universal concepts that fully capture the qualities of compositions. But to describe a design with a strong composition, we can use ideas such as unity and integrity. When a design evokes a sense of unity and integrity, it is felt to be a composition: something held together as a whole, with a purpose and intention. We feel that the design has an integrity that cannot easily be changed, and this integrity then influences our whole approach towards the design.

A strong composition makes it possible for almost anyone to recognize it, or at least to be unconsciously influenced by it and to

277

adjust one's approach to the design. A strong composition has real influence on the people responsible for managing the design, since they recognize the composition and may even feel compelled to adapt to its strong composition, when making changes to the design.

On the other hand, a weak composition may invite any number of changes—local, global, radical, or small—without any consideration of the existing composition at all. This happens because a weak composition is not easily detected and therefore may not affect the people responsible for managing the design. Regardless of whether it's strong or weak, all designs do have a composition that will influence the user's conception and use of the design. It may even be the case that the strength of a design's composition can be measured in relation to the skill and effort needed to detect and understand it.

It's not always easy to decide if a composition will be successful as an innovation—something that has become a *real* part of the world. A design with a strong composition—but situated in a context for which it was not designed, or that has radically changed over time—can be obstructed from becoming a successful design innovation expressive of soul. But if that design is placed within a suitable context, it will find stability and endurance even in the midst of a complex and changing environment. This situation often appears in urban design, where design judgments are made that affect both the life of each single building, as well as the overall design of a neighborhood, community or district.

A very strong building design can influence design possibilities in an entire neighborhood. In an area of buildings with weak compositions, almost anything can be put up. At the same time, the area may lack a sense of wholeness and stability. The same scenario holds true for weak and strong compositions designed for information systems and organizations. Strong contexts for design attract strong compositions. Well-designed systems invite well-designed subsystems. A great information system or a great organizational system sets standards and expectations against which proposed future designs or redesigns will be measured. Poorly formed contexts drag in poorly executed designs.

Yet, no matter how well designed, almost every composition will eventually have a *breakdown* at the material or pattern level. The essential character or soul of a particular design may be enduring, but there is vulnerability at pre-compositional levels of resolution. Why? Because when changes are made to a design's fundamental elements, materials or patterns of relationships—no matter whether it's an artifact, process, or system—it affects the entire composition. Compositions are affected even by the smallest changes that occur over time. At a certain point, as a result of these changes, the composition will not hold. The design will have a compositional breakdown. This means that the composition will no longer have impact on the people using or managing the system with the same kind of emergent qualities as present before.

When we reach the point of composition breakdown, we have a very sensitive and unstable system to deal with. Even small changes will create dramatic effects, for instance, when the structure of a carefully composed learning process is constantly modified by small changes. These interventions may consist of minor alterations to a delineated process, which someone found difficult to implement within the given structure and were therefore implemented as temporary solutions, based on different requirements than the original specifications. As these temporary solutions accumulate, they eventually threaten the basic structure of the original design. Ultimately, this learning process will become too difficult to understand, because it is no longer based on one integrated and congruent pedagogical idea. This problem will restrict the potential strategies for handling the design as a whole and will radically change our perception of the design. Character, soul and composition will be distorted or may even disappear.

But this fundamental breakdown is not inevitable. It is possible both to maintain a composition's basic integrity and to repair its constitutive elements. A careful and intimate understanding of a composition's essential character will guide new changes, so as to preserve and maybe even improve the composition's ability to be a conveyor of soul. To succeed, compositional refinement and modification demands earnest design effort and skill, which is why it sometimes seems easier to let the old composition die off completely, in order to create something new from scratch.

What we have shown here is that soul is not an autonomous, abstract property of a design. The way we define ensoulment and character makes it intimately interconnected all the way from the details of material to its contextual appropriateness. To ensoul is to carefully attend to all these levels and aspects of a composition.

One aspect of ensoulment that is sometimes used as a measure of quality is apparent *timelessness*. Given that with the passage of enough time, everything is temporary, timelessness is not about time-based considerations. A timeless design can be understood as a design that is not only appreciated at a specific time and in a specific place, for a specific purpose; it is also a design that is valued by people in different times and places, because it represents enduring and commonly held human values. Timeless designs are evaluated for qualities of excellence and virtue. They are not valued because of their temporal appearance in the world. They are not examples of the *latest* fashion in clothes, cars or art movements. They do not become *old* fashioned with the passage of time. They stand outside of the realm of time. In this way they express the qualities that spiritual traditions seek to find through religious experience.

How is this timeless quality possible, if we have defined the expression of soul in a design to be the manifestation of a resonance between its value and meaning, in a *specific* or *particular* situation? One answer could be that the evoked presence of soul in a timeless design isn't merely because it resonates with a particular situation: in addition, it resonates with something more enduring, more constant and more eternal. What could this larger, eternal reference be? There are several possibilities. A traditional option could, of course, be found in religion. If a design can be understood in relationship to the structure or content of religious beliefs, it will have some of the stability of the religion itself. In today's society, we can also imagine using cultural heritage as a general reference. However, the most powerful reference today, which evokes timelessness, is the notion of the natural or nature.

Timeless design, in this context, can be seen as a design that has values and meaning which relate to something in our society that is very stable over time and outside of time. Given this prerequisite, timeless designs are immensely difficult to realize. A designer is typically too preoccupied or influenced by contemporary styles, fashions, fads and 'the latest' theories (flavor-of-the-month). To be able to understand contemporary ideals, as well as relate them to something that is less temporal, is probably a task too difficult to be done as an intentional act. The timelessness that we see in some designs is more or less a result of either luck or exceptional skills.

In a society like our own, which depends heavily on its designs, we need both that which is timeless and that which is meant only for the present desired end. We need timeless designs to remind us of those values that are unchanging, common and eternal. Timeless designs bear witness to our common humanity, from which we form our cultures and other diverse expressions of valued creations. The design approach is a lifelong challenge to create designs that some day might be appreciated as timeless. To ensoul a design in a way that serves people now and far into the future is something worth striving for.

So, an ensouled design seems to be a complex combination of knowledge, skill, circumstances and luck. But, what happens when we encounter an already existing design? Can we observe or experience the soul in it? Does it matter how we approach the design? Do we need any special knowledge, skill, procedures, or preconditions to be able to see the soul of that design?

The answer is yes. But a purely analytical approach is not the best way to illuminate a design's soul. They—design souls— seem to be ephemeral creatures, not easily analyzed into constituent parts and functions. Instead each design composition has to be understood as a whole, as *one* unified experience. James Hillman has richly developed this idea of unity and the place of the soul. He claims the natural domain of reality is not the only place where this unity exists.

> Not only animals and plants are ensouled as in the Romantic vision, but soul is given with each thing, God-given things of nature and man-made things of the street.

> J. Hillman (1992)

282

According to the 'Romantic vision', referenced by Hillman, there is only one means for accessing original unity and that is through the instrumentality of the *immediate experience*. For some thinkers, the immediate experience is believed to be a way to reach the almost magical, hidden dimensions of our everyday world. To see the world holistically, as a 'divine' wholeness, where every single aspect of the totality of experience is also seen as a member of, or even the same thing as, 'the' divine. Still, there are many other ways of interpreting immediate experience. For instance, it could be thought of as a different form of rationality or intuitive knowledge.

Hillman is convinced that designs themselves can be understood as carriers of something we, as observers and users, actually experience (similar to Nozick's definition of value). To Hillman it is not a question of simple projection. It is not a question of total subjectivism, or relativism. A design carries something that strongly influences us, something that affects our imagination.

> This sudden illumination of the thing does not, however, depend on its formal, aesthetics proportion, which makes it 'beautiful'; it depends rather upon the movements of the *anima mundi* animating her images and affecting our imagination. The soul of the thing corresponds or coalesces with ours.
>
> J. Hillman (1992)

It is not about the superficial surface of the design, neither is it about its depth. The surface and the depth create an emergent image. We experience an artifact as ensouled when its image shows a sufficient complexity. "An object bears witness to itself in the image it offers, and its depth lies in the complexities of this image" (Hillman 1992).

283

It is in this complexity that we can see and experience the careful-ness and concern that has been devoted to the composition and the production of the design. When Hillman writes that "The soul of the thing corresponds or coalesces with ours," it is similar to our notion of the resonance between the design and its specific situation, in which we are unquestionably featured.

The idea of immediate experience tells us that designs have to be approached as a whole. They must be experienced as creators of com-plex and rich images. This does not mean that we just wait around for a design to jump out of its seat and grab our full attention. To be able to read and see the soul of a design, we must pay the same kind of attention in our examination of it as the designer did in the design process.

Carefulness and concern for both the details and overall composi-tion are things we look for in good designs. It is, in part, how we recognize ensouled artifacts. To make an artifact soulful demands time and effort. We need to 'put our soul' into the design. But what is also needed is a similar devotion from the beholder or user. There is sym-metry between the carefulness needed from the designer and the user. Hillman (1992) refers this careful attention and examination of artifacts to the concept of *notitia*, when he writes: "Attention to the qualities of things resurrects the old idea of notitia as a primary activity of the soul. Notitia refers to that capacity to form true notions of things from attentive noticing."

As designers, we're all familiar with the situation in which we have designed something, really putting our hearts and souls into the work, and the work is not taken seriously. Even complimentary critiques, such as, "that looks good," or "that is a nice design," are basically worthless to us, if we suspect that it is not based on a careful examination or real concern. What we are looking for from those judging our design is *authentic attention*.

Authentic attention means that the idea of the ensouled design is taken seriously. Authentic attention is a more demanding process than we usually ascribe to our everyday activities. Although we frequently experience it in other fields, such as art, music, or in our relation to nature and each other, we're less likely to experience it with design. It means that in order to fully and authentically appreciate the essential character and quality of a design, adequate and appropriate time and effort must be devoted to the task.

So, let's recap what we know about the ensoulment process. It appears abundantly clear that there are no guidelines, no techniques and no straightforward methods on how to ensoul your designs. The entire process presupposes the utilization of much energy, time and careful attention. In addition, it is not enough to focus on the surface appearance of designs, the visual shape or image of the artifact. There must be more involved. Ensoulment is about wholeness and composition, as well as value and meaning. It is about carefulness when attending to details and relationships. To ensoul a design—in a way that attracts attention and appreciation—demands a respect for the materials, the structure, the shape and its social dimensions. It also demands courage (Grudin, 1990; May, 1975). To design is to interject something risky into the world—to create the *not-yet-existing* is chancy.

Another aspect of ensouled designs is related to the notion of caring. As designers we must design for the entire life span of the design. Someone is required to be responsible for the well being of the design throughout its life. The designer can facilitate this by creating ensouled designs. To do this requires that the designer strives for sensibility of the whole—the internal unified coherence of how it

285

relates to a specific situation—for this is what makes it feel as if it were 'timeless'. When we ensoul our work, we also make it into something loved and precious; when something is precious to us, we want to care for it. Beloved artifacts give us pleasure when we use them. They even bring pleasure when we're simply in close proximity to them. This is true for all manner of designs—the soulful organization, car, cup, toy, or learning process. They all become precious to us, if through authentic attention and notitia, we find them soulful. That makes us want to take care of them. Thus, by ensouling our designs, we create the desire in others to care for the design's future use and development.

The idea of ensouled design has another, important meaning. We live in a world of designed, artificial environments. Within this artificial world, we have created organizations, work processes, procedures and rules. To live in such environments, especially if they are constantly changing, takes time and energy. If these environments are without soul, it makes people tired, it drains us of energy. An ensouled environment, on the other hand, *evokes life*. When we encounter ensouled designs, we are energized. We feel that our own souls are filled with splendor. To take part in the ongoing design of reality is therefore a task of ever-greater responsibility. Since it's not just a question of creating a functioning, ethical and aesthetic environment, but also involves creating a reality that can either give people energy and hope, or make their lives poorer in spirit.

> Once we recognize, however, that the need for beauty must be met, but that scenic, physical nature is not the only place it can be met, we would take the soul back into our own hands, realizing that what happens with it is less given and more man-made

through our work with it in the actual world by making that actual world reflect the soul's need for beauty.

J. Hillman (1992)

The creation of ensouled designs not only affects the user, but also the designer. The act of creating ensouled compositions infuses life-enhancing energy into the designer, as much as it does the client. To be given the opportunity to discharge design intentions in a manner that assures a soulful outcome is one of the designer's most satisfying rewards. It feels great! On the other hand, when you are not able to work in a soul-full design way, a designer's energy is drained and the very splendor inherent in designing disappears. What remains is merely a process of adapting and compromising to given conditions and predetermined outcomes. The deeper meaning of being a designer vanishes.

When we start to understand design as a process of ensoulment, when we become aware that every design process and composition ultimately contributes to a larger whole, we—as designers—begin to realize more fully our responsibility to the planet as a whole. We become aware that every design process, every composition, contributes to this larger design. To be a part of this endlessly unfolding process is both wonderful and terrifying, as every design—no matter how small or presumably insignificant—either contributes to that wholeness or makes it less so. The responsibility is there. The challenge is clear—expedient lifelessness or splendor?

V. CHARACTER AND COMPETENCE

In this book we have presented what we see as a basis for a design culture. It is our attempt to help forge a crucible for design competence and a new way of approaching intentional change. Designers need an environment that is supportive of their work. The design process requires defined limits and space within which one's ideas can unfold safely. We have also learned, though, that simply having a protective environment is not enough. If our endeavors are to be successful, *The Design Way* reminds us that both a design culture (one that defines the general limits) and a design context (one that defines the particular limits) need to be securely in place before we can begin. Hopefully, the composition of ideas presented in this book has, in some way, evoked a deeper understanding of what is at the heart of design and being a designer.

We would like to take the opportunity now to comment on, at least briefly, what it means for an individual designer to develop a more personal understanding of these ideas and to think and practice in a designerly way.

The single-most important guarantee of design excellence is the presence of *design character*. A young designer can rattle off basic design tenets until he or she is worn out. However, not until design's core values have begun to reside within—to be embodied in—his or her *character*, will that designer be able to practice bona fide design—especially design that is *soul-full*. Design takes place in the real particular, which means there are no universal truths, no generalized solutions; design resides in the realm of the ultimate particular. Designing is about handling complexity and richness, tensions and contradictions, possibilities and limits, all of which require design to be a matter of making good judgments. You may remember that we've defined judgment as 'knowing', based on knowledge inseparable from the 'knower'. Lastly, design is about composition, and composition never emerges from prescriptive rules or principles, it is always an act of judgment. All in all, design as described here emanates from, and points to, the individual designer's core of being—his or her character.

Now, this doesn't mean we're arguing that design is such an individualistic process that it resides in the heroic tradition of the lone wolf. Design has always been, and will continue to be, collaborative at its core; even if that collaboration only includes one designer and one client. Design activities are typically carried out in groups, with many roles involved in complex relationships. Still, the bearer of cultural norms, and the source of design imagination and agency, will always be the individual. It is the individual designer who has the responsibility to act in a design-driven way; to initiate and develop a design culture; foster design behavior in other stakeholders and in society at large; mentor design colleagues and form design contexts in the particular.

This leads us right back to the designer and his or her character. The big question then becomes—how is it possible to develop one's design character?

The process of learning to design is different from most traditional forms of education, which are based on academic disciplines, or professional areas of expertise. Designers need to be educated with the understanding that they are expected to produce *unexpected* outcomes. This concept is quite foreign to those who train most agents of change, where students are taught to produce expected outcomes, because of an assumed logical relationship between educational input and predetermined performance competence. Although this goal is important to many human endeavors, it is just part of the expectation of design, or designers, and not even the most critical part.

Keep in mind that every designer does have a specific field of expertise. In this field the designer will have a basic and advanced education in the craft, skills, materials, principles, language, styles, traditions, methods and techniques specific to that field. These fields are usually defined as professional areas or disciplines, such as: industrial design, architecture, information design, software design, urban design, organizational design, educational design, instructional design, etc. This is by no means a complete list, since the designer may come from a self-organized community of practice as well. The ideas we've presented do not change the need for factual knowledge and skill sets. Field-specific, professional competence is always necessary. However, it needs to be maintained within the context of deeper, more abstract understandings of design, understandings that are appropriate across diverse fields of application.

291

Even though the specifics of a particular design field are important, the more universal ideas associated with the development and maintenance of a culture of design, as presented in this book, have significant consequences for design learning and require their own particular approach. Rather than offer specifics, we have constructed a platform for reflection and action that can cross the boundaries of any particular design field.

But again, let's get back to the issue of character. Becoming a designer is not a genetic gift. Design can be learned as well as taught. As in many other areas of life, talent and personality play a role, but education, training and motivation can contribute significantly to the development of a good designer. The time and effort required differ, in the same way they would in any other area of life. Therefore, the underlying possibility of designing is open to everyone.

Given that, we'd like to present a hierarchy of essential designer qualities (see Fig. V-1). These 7 *c's* spell out the qualities a student needs to navigate in order to be a good designer. Each of these qualities is given value by the categories listed above it. For example, knowledge is of little use without the ability to act on it. The ability to act, to create change, is of little use in design if there is no ability to produce or make something. The ability to produce or make something is of little consequence, without the ability to learn how and what to produce. The capacity to learn is given value and purpose through courage, which in turn, is given meaning through systemic or holistic connection.

These seven essential qualities should be constantly examined and reflected upon and intentionally developed by the individual designer. Since this book is not focused on design education as such, we will not elaborate on the 7 *c's* here, but it is important to understand that

292

formalized strategies for learning play an essential part in the development of design character. Everyone comes into the developmental process with certain designerly qualities, more or less well developed, with other qualities in need of greater focused attention. A simple reflective examination and exploration of these internal design qualities by the designer and his/her peers, mentors and teachers, in relation to the designer's professional goals, will help determine where further development is required. This kind of reflection provides the designer with clarity around one's own design strengths and weaknesses.

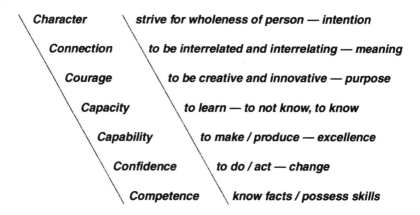

Fig. V-1 Hierarchy of Designer Qualities—the 7 c's

Designers must learn to make compositions. This is a fundamental design skill, but not something typically taught at the core of traditional professional learning models. Most of the learning models prevalent today are based on an analytic approach to 'knowing'.

Taking reality apart categorically does this. Reductive, analytic and logical skills are held as core competencies and are expected to be both trainable and testable. Even within traditional design fields, the focus of learning is not on holistic composition skills, but on material or craft skills. Designer education must focus on the act of systemic composition. Because composition is about the creation of wholes, there is a need for *fusion learning*, in addition to critical or analytic learning. Fusion learning is learning how to unify and compose, so as to create intentional, emergent properties.

Design learning takes place in a variety of settings, using many different methods, based on the expected outcome of what is to be learned. Design knowing can be distinguished as either focused on the abstract universal, or the concrete particular, or as a relationship between the personal and the organizational (see Fig. V-2).

Among these different settings, it is possible to construct a variety of approaches to design learning. On the organizational side—in combination with the universal—we find a more traditional approach to education, where generalized knowledge and skills are presented to a group of people at the same time (usually through lectures and demonstrations). In the organizational and particular quadrant, customized approaches to design action suitable for a specific environment, organization, or group are presented. For example organizational development (OD) programs are typical of this area. This form of education is often labeled as 'training' in the workplace.

Within the personal and the particular quadrant of design practice, we find design judgment in action. The case study method used by schools of management and law schools is an example of how particular types of judgment—like navigational judgment—are taught and learned. When a person is focused solely on the particular, there are no general rules or guidelines that are applicable. No general or abstract universal knowledge fits exactly and often not even closely. This is because the particular situation is unique, requiring insights particular to the design at hand. In dealing with the ultimate particular or concrete particular, judgment needs to be brought in. This is where design judgment is developed through coaching and mentoring. In the final quadrant, that of the personal and the universal, the focus is on the universality of being a person. Education in this realm requires that your fundamental design character be challenged by new insights, new ideas and new experience in relationship to other peoples' experience; in order to assure that individual experience is given meaning as 'common' experience in lieu of it being strictly personal.

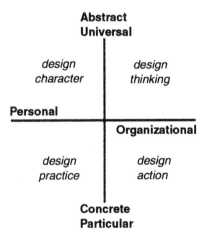

Fig. V-2 Design Learning

Just as every design project must be done in relation to the particular requirements and circumstances of the job, developing one's design ability calls for different educational approaches, depending on what is desired to be learned. There is a time and place for all four domains. The *design of the designer* is brought about through successfully integrating the universal and particular, as well as the personal and organizational in an over-all composition for learning.

A designer's character evolves at a snail-like pace, staying remarkably recognizable over time. That is why its development demands ongoing attention. Character is not something that can be changed quickly. A person's character is inclusive of their *daemon*, meaning the essence of soul that we are born with, which evokes our 'calling' in life. The daemon constitutes who we are from the beginning of our lives (Hillman, 1996).

Hillman presents a way to understand the complex relationship between who we are when we are born, and how we change and develop over time. He explains that to carefully reflect on who we are, in our soul, is a lifelong exercise. It is an exercise that is both painful and rewarding. It is through such continuous reflection—on who we are, what our calling is, what we can do with our life—that we create the basis of our character. For Hillman, our character is (even when stable and deeply rooted) open to change in intentional ways. As designers, we have an obligation to continuously examine, challenge and influence our design character. To act in this way is not simply a matter of going about one's design activities, but also involves reflecting, proactively, on the relationship between design character and design competence.

As stated earlier, design learning includes everything from gaining specific skills to design character. Like the layers of an onion, the designer slowly begins to acquire new and deeper levels of understanding (see Fig V-3).

1ST ORDER— BASICS
TRUTHS
FACTS
FOREGROUND – CONTEXT
BACKGROUND – ENVIRONMENT

2ND ORDER— SYSTEMS
PATTERNS
ASSEMBLIES
ARCHETYPES

3RD ORDER— PROTOCOLS/LIMITS/SPACE
ORDERING PRINCIPLES
ORGANIZING DISPOSITIONS
FRAMES – BOUNDARIES
CONTAINERS
CRUCIBLES

4TH ORDER—EMERGENCE/FORM
COMPOUNDS
COMPOSITIONS
WHOLES

5TH ORDER— GUARANTOR-OF-DESIGN
TELOS
g.o.d.

6TH ORDER—GUARANTOR OF DESTINY
G.O.D.

Fig. V-3 Hierarchy of Learning

Each order of emergence has its own epistemological forms and means of cognition, perception and skill development. The approaches to learning, the kinds of knowledge and understanding that emerge and the commitment of time and effort required, change with each level. The disciplinary, academic traditions are to be found primarily in the first order of learning, as presented in this model. Although other areas of study have hundreds of different orders of learning, those presented here are grounded in the tradition of design. Very few formal design curriculums encompass more than two or three of the basic levels presented here. However, a good and hopefully wise, designer must authentically engage with them all. This requires that he or she become a self-directed, life-long learner.

As we have stated many times, to design is to intentionally change the world. Thus, every designer is a *leader* in the truest and fullest sense of the word, because every design process is about leading the world into a new reality—a place we have never seen or been before. Design is always moving into the unknown and we can never really 'undo' a design. Even if the specific artifact or design is removed, the design has already made an imprint on the world as an idea or image. People have been changed, probably in both their thinking and their actions. Materials and energy have been used in a way that is never recoverable. Therefore, to be a designer requires an intrepid nature, as such a person opens up portals to new realities and provokes the world into moving into the new unknown. This type of person must be a leader in the most profound sense.

Conversely, a leader is always a designer, since a leader's role is, by definition, leading people into new realities. Good leaders are good designers and vice versa. This reciprocal relationship holds true even when a designer acts in service to a client. The designer still has the obligation to open up access to new ideas, new realities, all based on the desiderata of the client. As there is no *guarantor-of-design*—except the character of the designer—there is no way to escape this leadership role. This added responsibility of leadership may sometimes be difficult for designers to embrace, but it is a very real part of the designer's calling.

The Design Way is focused on making the case for forging a crucible for a design culture and making a case for a design-driven way to approach the world. Design thinking and design activity needs to be held in a cultural container—a social crucible—that provides oversight as well as nurturing, supporting and protecting the work of its designers and all those who benefit from design activities. The crucible—as a container for creative and innovative work—is not something that occurs naturally, but needs to be developed, continuously renewed and eventually replaced. Within a healthy design culture, designers, their champions, clients and other stakeholders fulfill this function.

It is important to remember that design is a choice, one among many triggers that drives intentional behavior (see Fig. V-4). Depending on how this choice is made, its purpose, outcomes and consequences will vary significantly and have a major influence on what can be accomplished. Choosing the design approach requires that a context and environment—which is congruent with design behavior—be in place. In other words, a design crucible must be formed. Within this container, which defines the limits and possibilities of design activity, design competence is an essential and pragmatic means of engaging with the crucible.

One of the benefits of choosing a design approach is that all parties have 'bought into' design, as its own tradition. Without an awareness of this initial precondition, any creative or innovative actions upon the world will lack the accountability that comes with a design contract because of its fundamental service relationship. When designers are socially and culturally legitimized, design becomes a recognized and valued approach to change by society at large (i.e., a design culture).

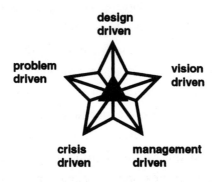

Fig. V-4 Drivers of Action

In the absence of a design tradition within a design culture, designers are often forced into other traditions of intentional action, in order to find enabling support for their work. There is the growing realization that this 'borrowing' does not serve or fit the essential nature of design and that the core activities of the design process are not efficiently or effectively supported under these conditions. Design and its design-driven behavior are fatally restricted because the borrowed approaches do not match the undertaking and critical elements are missing. Of those elements that are present, many are inappropriate for design-related tasks. Designing must be supported by a design tradition composed of design related activities.

A well-nourished design culture allows us to become self-consciously reflective as world creators. The implications of such a culture extend well beyond the confines of this book. Among such implications is the recognition of a new form of democracy, based on design-inspired relationships of service. Another implication is the concept of inclusiveness, which embraces difference, diversity and complexity with all their contradictions. The design tradition is, by nature, inclusive of other modes of inquiry and action. In design, there are no 'science wars' or 'cultural wars'. When there are conflicts of this nature it means that the true or ideal, rather than the real, has become the foundation for inquiry and action. This means that design is no longer the focus. Design deals with the real, which by definition includes all possible aspects of reality.

Design competence allows individuals to become causal agents of the real world. This competence is an embodiment of the foundations and fundamentals presented in this book and subsequently acted upon with the values and principles of a design culture. Anyone who so chooses can become design competent, as can any collective of like-minded individuals. Design competency asserts the capacity to create a design crucible—through the positive presence of a design culture—thus creating the potential for cross-catalytic cause and effect functionality.

Design touches nearly every aspect of our real world. This is something that we can't ignore, or pretend isn't the case. We must come to terms with our own ingenuity, authority and responsibility. In *The Design Way*, we hope we have presented you with an introduction to a powerful and important way of working and being in the world.

301

Design has done great service for humanity, as well as great harm. Possessing design competence, the ability to engage so significantly in the world, is the essence of being a designer and a human being. Pursuing the design intentions and purposes presented in this book is a life-long commitment to one of the most important design processes you can engage in—it is the design of your own life.

References

Ackoff, R. L. (1978). *The Art of Problem Solving*. New York, NY. John Wiley & Sons, Inc.

Ackoff, R. L. & Emery, F. E. (1972). *On Purposeful Systems*. Seaside, CA. Intersystems Publications.

Arnheim, R. (1995). Sketching and the Psychology of Design. Margolin, V. (*et al.*, Eds.). *The Idea of Design*. Cambridge, MA. The MIT Press.

Banathy, B. H. (1996). *Designing Social Systems in a Changing World*. New York, NY. Plenum Press.

Bertalanffy, L. v. (1968). *General Systems Theory: Foundations, Development, Applications*. New York, NY. George Braziller, Inc.

Buchanan, R. & Margolin, V. (Eds.) (1995). *Discovering Design: Explorations in Design Studies*. Chicago, IL. The University of Chicago Press.

Campbell, J. (1968). *The Hero with a Thousand Faces*. Princeton, NJ. Princeton University Press.

Checkland, P. (1981). *Systems Theory, Systems Practice*. New York, NY. John Wiley & Sons, Inc.

Churchman, C. W. (1961). *Prediction and Optimal Decision: Philosophical Issues of a Science of Values*. Englewood Cliffs, NJ. Prentice-Hall.

Churchman, C. W. (1971). *The Design of Inquiring Systems: Basic Concepts of Systems and Organization*. New York, NY. Basic Books, Inc.

Churchman, C. W. (1979). *The Systems Approach and Its Enemies*. New York, NY. Basic Books, Inc.

Collingwood, R. G. (1939). *An Autobiography*. Oxford, UK. Clarendon Press.

Crosby, A. W. (1997). *The Measure of Reality: Quantification and Western Society, 1250-1600*. New York, NY. Cambridge University Press.

Cross, N. (2001). Designerly Ways of Knowing: Design Discipline Versus Design Science. *Design Studies*, 17(No. 3), Summer 2001, 49-55.

Csikszentmihali, M. (1990). *Flow: The Psychology of Optimal Experience; Steps toward Enhancing the Quality of Life*. New York, NY. Harper & Row.

303

Dewey, J. (1910). *How We Think*. Amherst, New York. Prometheus Books.

Dunne, J. (1993). *Back to the Rough Ground: 'Phronesis' and 'Techné' in Modern Philosophy and in Aristotle*. Notre Dame, IN. University of Notre Dame Press.

Follett, M. P. (1930). *Creative Experience*. New York, NY. Longmans, Green and Co.

Gharajedaghi, J. (1999). *Systems Thinking: Managing Chaos and Complexity; A Platform for Designing Business Architecture*. Boston, MA. Butterworth Heinmann.

Grudin, R. (1990). *The Grace of Great Things: Creativity and Innovation*. New York, NY. Ticknor & Fields.

Herrigel, E. (1953). *Zen in the Art of Archery*. New York, NY. Pantheon Books/Random House.

Hillman, J. (1992). *The Thought of the Heart & the Soul of the World*. Dallas, TX. Spring Publications, Inc.

Hillman, J. (1996). *The Soul's Code: In Search of Character and Calling*. New York, NY. Random House.

Hillman, J. (1999). *The Force of Character and the Lasting Life*. New York, NY. Random House.

Huxley, A. (1944). *The Perennial Philosophy*. New York, NY. Harper and Row.

Isaacs, W. (1999). *Dialogue and the Art of Thinking Together: A Pioneering Approach to Communicating in Business and in Life*. New York, NY. Currency Doubleday.

James, W. (1975). *Pragmatism, a New Name for Some Old Ways of Thinking, and The Meaning of Truth: A Sequel to Pragmatism*. Cambridge, MA. Harvard University Press.

Janlert, L-E. & Stolterman, E. (1997). The character of things. *Design Studies*, 18 (No. 3), July (1997): 297-314.

Jantsch, E. (1975). *Design for Evolution: Self-Organization and Planning in the Life of Human Systems*. New York, NY. George Braziller, Inc.

Kant, I. (1790). *Critique of Judgement.* Translation by W. Pluhar, published 1987. Indianapolis. Hackett Publishing Company.

Kuhn, T. (1962). *The Structure of Scientific Revolutions.* Chicago, IL. University of Chicago Press.

Löwgren, J. & Stolterman, E. (1999). Developing IT Design Ability through Repertoires and Contextual Product Semantics. *Digital Creativity,* 9 (No. 4): 223-237.

Makkreel, R. A. (1990). *Imagination and Interpretation in Kant; the Hermeneutical Import of the Critique of Judgment.* Chicago, IL. The University of Chicago Press.

Margolin, V. & Buchanan, R. (Eds.) (1995). *The Idea of Design.* Cambridge, MA. The MIT Press.

May, R. (1975). *The Courage to Create.* New York, NY. W. W. Norton & Co., Inc.

Nelson, H. G. (1987). Other Than Chance and Necessity: Intention and Purpose by Design. *European Journal of Operational Research,* 30(No. 3): 356-358.

Nelson, H. G. (1994). The Necessity of Being "Undisciplined" and "Out-of-Control": Design Action and Systems Thinking. *Performance Improvement Quarterly,* 7(No. 3): 22-29.

Norman, D. (1993). *Things That Make Us Smart: Defending Human Attributes in the Age of the Machine.* New York, NY. Addison-Wesley.

Nozick, R. (1989). *The Examined Life — Philosophical Meditations.* New York, NY. Touchstone Book.

Nussbaum, M. C. (1990). *Love's Knowledge: Essays on Philosophy and Literature.* New York, NY. Oxford University Press.

Nussbaum, M. C. (1997). *Cultivating Humanity: A Classical Defense of Reform in Liberal Education.* Cambridge, MA. Harvard University Press.

Pirsig, R. M. (1981). *Zen and the Art of Motorcycle Maintenance.* New York, NY. Bantam New Age Books.

Platts, M. J. (1997). Competence: The Virtue of Maturity. *Proceedings from the 6th Symposium on Automated Systems Based on Human Skill,* Slovenia.

Remen, R. N. (1996). In the Service of Life. *Noetic Sciences Review,* Spring, 1996.

Rittel, H. (1972). On the Planning Crisis: Systems Analysis of the 'First and Second Generations'. *Bedrifts Okonomen* (Norway)(No. 8): 390-396.

Rittel, H. W. J. & Webber, M. M., (1974). Dilemmas in a General Theory of Planning. *Design Research and Methods,* 8(No. 1): 31-39.

Rorty, A. (2001). *The Many Faces of Evil — Historical Perspectives.* London, UK. Routledge.

Schön, D. A. (1983). *The Reflective Practitioner.* New York, NY. Basic Books.

Schön, D. A. & Rein, M. (1994). *Frame Reflection — Towards the Resolution of Intractable Policy Controversies.* New York, NY. Basic Books.

Searle, J. R. (1983). *Intentionality: An Essay in the Philosophy of Mind.* New York, NY. Cambridge University Press.

Simon, H. (1969). *The Science of the Artificial.* Cambridge, MA. MIT Press.

Snow, C. P. (1959). *The Two Cultures.* Cambridge, UK. Cambridge University Press.

Stolterman, E. (1999). The Design of Information Systems — Parti, Formats and Sketching. *Information Systems Journal,* 9(No. 1), January 1999.

Sunstein, C. R. (2001). *Designing Democracy — What Constitutions Do.* Oxford, UK. Oxford University Press.

Toynbee, A. J. (1948). *A Study of History* (Vols. 1-12). Oxford, UK. Oxford University Press.

Trainor, R. (2001). *Befriending Our Desires.* Lecture at Seattle University, May 1st, 2001, Seattle, WA.

Tufte, E. R. (1983). *The Visual Display of Quantitative Information.* Cheshire, CT. Graphics Press.

Tufte, E. R. (1990). *Envisioning Information.* Cheshire, CT. Graphics Press.

Vickers, G. (1995). *The Art of Judgment: A Study of Policy Making.* Thousand Oaks, CA. Sage Publications.

Wittgenstein, L. (1963). *Philosophical Investigations.* (Translated by G.E.M. Anscombe). Oxford, UK. Basil Blackwell.

Zsambok, C. E. & Klein, G. (1997). *Naturalistic Decision Making.* Mahwah, NJ. Lawrence Erlbaum Associates.

307

Index

309

Dr. **Harold G. Nelson** is the President and Co-founding Director of the Advanced Design Institute. Dr. Nelson works as a consultant to corporations, governmental agencies, international organizations and educational institutions in the area of Organizational Design Competence. He is an Affiliated Associate Professor of Mechanical Engineering and an Extended Faculty in the Information School at the University of Washington where his focus is on teaching and research in systems design. He is Past-President of the International Society for Systems Science. For over 12 years Dr. Nelson was the head of the graduate programs in social and organizational systems design at Antioch University. He received his Ph.D. in Social Systems Design from the University of California at Berkeley. He is a registered architect in the State of California.

Dr. **Erik Stolterman** is the Vice President and Co-founding Director of the Advanced Design Institute. Dr. Stolterman is a Professor in the Department of Informatics, at Umeå University in Sweden. His main research is in Information Technology and Society, Information Systems Design, Philosophy of Design, and Philosophy of Technology. Apart from his academic and scholarly work Dr. Stolterman engages in consulting with organizations and companies. He received his Ph.D. in Informatics from Umeå University.